PACIFIC COOPERATION
AND DEVELOPMENT

PACIFIC
COOPERATION
AND DEVELOPMENT

Edited by
George Kozmetsky
Hiroshi Matsumoto
Raymond W. Smilor

PRAEGER

New York
Westport, Connecticut
London

No Texas State funds were used in the preparation of this book.

Library of Congress Cataloging-in-Publication Data

Pacific cooperation and development.

Papers presented at the 1987 Global Community
Forum, held in Apia, Western Samoa.
  Bibliography: p.
  Includes index.
  1. Oceania—Economic conditions—Congresses
2. Technological innovations—Economic aspects—
Oceania—Congresses. 3. Appropriate technology—
Oceania—Congresses. 4. Oceania—Economic policy—
Congresses. 5. Oceania—Economic integration—
Congresses. I. Kozmetsky, George. II. Matsumoto,
Hiroshi. III. Smilor, Raymond W. IV. Global Community
Forum (1987 : Apia, Western Samoa)
HC681.P283   1988   330.99   88-15272

ISBN 0-275-93095-5 (alk. paper)

Library of Congress Catalog Card Number: 88-15272
ISBN: 0-275-93095-5

First published in 1988

Praeger Publishers, One Madison Avenue, New York, NY 10010
A division of Greenwood Press, Inc.

Printed in the United States of America

The paper used in this book complies with the
Permanent Paper Standard issued by the National
Information Standards Organization (Z39.48-1984).

10 9 8 7 6 5 4 3 2 1

Contents

Foreword

The first conference, Global Community Forum '81 was organized in Kobe port island of Japan, a new, man-made addition to the surface of the globe. Its theme was "Asian Entrepreneurs and International Cooperation." Its purpose was to exchange participants' views on experiences with the managerial expertise of entrepreneurs in the development of their respective countries and organizations and to encourage new perspectives and practical efforts toward increased international cooperation.

The second Global Community Forum was held in 1984 in Kuala Lumpur, Malaysia, with "Southeast Asia and the Pacific Age" as the theme. The conference focused on Southeast Asia because this region had begun to experience dynamic growth and diversification. At the conference, the future of Pacific cooperation was emphasized because the center of activity of the globe was moving away from the Atlantic.

The concept of cooperation in the Pacific has been repeatedly discussed from the viewpoints of the advanced countries and those rimming the Pacific Ocean, but seldom from the perspectives and aspirations of the many island states that span the vast Pacific Ocean. Therefore, the third Global Community Forum met at Western Samoa in July 1987 to discuss "Pacific Cooperation and Development" not only by the peoples within the Pacific basin and the Pacific area but also on a realtime basis with interested citizens around the globe.

Significantly all the island states share a common environmental heritage and all are surrounded by Asia, the Americas and the Oceania. Therefore opinion molders gathered under a coconut roof--fale fono --in Apia where they could, in their individual capacity as global citizens, discuss and seek true Pacific cooperation and development that embraces the viewpoints of the peoples of the Pacific basin island states.

Global Community Forum '87 was designed to take full advantage of the latest communication technologies available. Global citizens around the world who were interested in the forum also participated, though not physically present, and gave their opinions while the conference was in progress.

It is our hope that the purposes as described above will be advanced through this publication of the proceedings of Global Community Forum '87 in Apia and will further reinforce the need for continued commitment and involvement toward Pacific cooperation and development from a global perspective.

Acknowledgments

We appreciate the many contributions of the people and organizations that helped make this book possible.

We are indebted to the organizations that sponsored and directed the international conference from which this book was developed. We wish to thank the Association for the Promotion of International Cooperation (APIC), Tokyo, Japan; the IC^2 Institute at The University of Texas at Austin; the Institute of Pacific Studies, the University of the South Pacific, Suva, Fiji; the National Institute for Research Advancement (NIRA), Tokyo, Japan; and the RGK Foundation, Austin, Texas. Each provided important resources and support for the conference and the book.

We are grateful to the Government of Western Samoa that served as host for the conference.

We appreciate the contributions of the supporting organizations: United Nations Development Program in New York City, and Nifco, Inc., Seiko Instruments, Inc., Seiko Epson Corporation, and Mitsubishi Electric Corporation in Tokyo.

In addition, we wish to thank the cooperating organizations for their support: *Asahi Newspaper*, Asahi Video Project, the *Japan Times*, the University of Hawaii, PEACESAT and TelAIR Project, the Hawaii Global TELEclass Project, Pacific International Co., Ltd., and Pacific Telecommunications Council.

We are especially grateful to a number of individuals without whose support, encouragement, direction, and active participation, this conference and book would not have been possible.

We wish to remember Ichiro Hattori, the late president of Seiko Instruments, Inc. and Seiko Epson Corporation, for his inspiration for and dedication to the purposes of the conference. We want to thank Yoshio Okawara, president of APIC and chairman of the conference steering committee, for his invaluable leadership. Toru Yano, vice-president of NIRA, provided key support and direction. C. S. Ananthan, senior advisor, Yuasa Battery Co., Ltd., Tokyo, assisted as rapporteur and editor on the Japan side. Norman George, minister of foreign affairs, Cook Islands, served as conference spokesman. Ronya Kozmetsky, president of the RGK Foundation, contributed to conference planning and development.

We are grateful to the other members of the steering committee: Ronald Crocombe, professor, University of the South Pacific; Le Tagaloa Pita, minister of economic affairs, Western Samoa; Aiono Fanaafi Le Tagaloa, member of parliament, Western Samoa; Toshiaki Ogasawara, president, NIFCO, Inc.; Saburo Okita, chairman, Institute for Domestic and International Policy Studies; Asesela Ravuvu, director, Institute of Pacific Studies, University of the South Pacific; Atsushi Shimokobe, president of NIRA; and Takeshi Watanabe, president, Japan Credit Rating Agency, Ltd.

Several others helped with administration and logistics for the conference. We appreciated the assistance of Hiroyasu Higuchi and Toshi Tsubo of APIC, and Cynthia Smith of the RGK Foundation.

We especially wish to thank Linda Teague of the IC^2 Institute for her excellent work in preparing the manuscript for publication. And we appreciate the copy-editing support of Nancy Richey, also of IC^2.

Praeger has been an outstanding press with which to work. We have benefited from the support and encouragement of George Zimmar and the assistance of Frank Welsch in the preparation of the manuscript.

We are grateful to each author who contributed to this volume, and to the academics, public officials, and business leaders who participated in the conference.

PACIFIC COOPERATION
AND DEVELOPMENT

Introduction

C. S. Ananthan

From the first day, as participants began arriving, it was evident to them that the South Pacific, once described by James H. Michener as a cluster of dream islands where troubled men seek solitude from the complexities of continental societies, is no longer isolated. While still preserving with dignity their traditional values and way of life, the island states of the South Pacific have become increasingly exposed to the exacerbating realities of international politics and economics from which they can no longer remain aloof or opt to remain isolated. Therefore, it was most appropriate that the Global Community Forum chose to hold its 1987 conference in the center of the Pacific basin, with the hope that its deliberations would radiate to all regions of the world, particularly the island states within the basin.

To make the foreign participants feel at home, the traditional Western Samoan hospitality was abundant. This warm hospitality and sincere friendship was helpful to the meeting and served to keep the exchange of thoughts under the coconut roof--Fale Fono ("conference house")--lowing in a manner conducive to Pacific cooperation and development, the theme subject to be deliberated on for two days by global citizens who were gathered there.

Feeling of oneness

The chairman of Global Community Forum 1987, Yoshio Okawara, in his opening address remarked that the participants as global citizens were gathered here with a "feeling of oneness" and asked that this be the motive force guiding them through the two days of deliberations to consolidate their thoughts for contributing to and enriching the global community. Indeed this "feeling of oneness" survived the heated discussions under the Fale Fono and elsewhere at informal gatherings during the two days of the conference.

The program for the first day delved deep into major topics of significant current importance and of major concern to the states of the Pacific islands. In particular, "Current experience and future potentials of economic development in the Pacific region" was taken up at the first session. The discussions following the presentations of the papers appeared to be focused heavily on trade imbalances between the two major economic powers in the free world, namely the United States and Japan. The increasing trend toward protectionism in the midst of impending recession was highlighted. On the other hand, the serious trauma of servicing debts, as faced by the developing nations, was raised as posing inevitable threats to any prospective thrust in Pacific cooperation and (economic) development . To compound the dismay already described, the subject of friction between civilizations was introduced. As to be expected, it was proposed that further serious studies by theoretical and pragmatic economists and sociopolitical reformists are "still" necessary to solve the myriad problems confronting cooperation and development in the Pacific areas.

While high-flown economic theories were being thrown about the conference tables, the distinguished global citizens from the far-flung but closely associated Pacific island states remained frightened and worried about a number of specific issues. Why was the coepora price falling and why did no one around the Pacific rim or outside appear to be concerned? Why was the introduction of the 200-mile Exclusive Economic Zone a significant worry to those around the Pacific rim and beyond? Was it because a sustainable yield of highly migratory species can be mismanaged? Why was it that so much attention had been suddenly directed to the tiny island states in the Pacific, with aid accompanied by managers to manage that aid? When the aid had ceased, the islanders were left with the burden of possibly servicing those aid debts, while their farm products could not be readily transported and if transported for export could only be sold for ridiculous prices. How was it that in the name of cooperation and development, they were encouraged to stretch out a hand toward the twenty-first century, with all its high technologies, yet keep the other hand vigorously working at deeply rooted ways of subsistence?

The warm, friendly, and highly knowledgeable global citizens of the Pacific island states did not remain silent listeners for long. With straight-forward logic, they responded. It was quite apparent that the highly industrialized nations face problems intrinsic to the very nature of their sophisticated service-oriented high-technology economies whereas a vast majority in the Pacific are in various stages of transience, be it economic, social, or political. Yet they are very much aware of and exposed to the world scenario of events and goods. The feeling of oneness initially expressed by the chairman in his opening address, prevailed throughout the heated discussions that ensued and helped bring to light the many practical means to put the machinery of Pacific cooperation and development to work.

A comprehensive plan

It was emphasized that a comprehensive plan, akin to the Marshall Plan, had to be worked out with creativity and specificity to meet the needs of the Pacific island states. But in discussing the friction between civilizations Toru Yano correctly pointed out that Japan's "internationalization must be designed not only to shift Japanese society into a more readily accessible system but to build a peaceful and reciprocal international order around Japan. The argument for internationalization should not be confined to that of how Japan ought to be, but must be broadened to encompass an international vision in which particular attention is paid to the security and development of Asia." (Yano, chapter 2) One could broaden these views to encompass the global community and for current discussions concerning the Pacific community. A comprehensive plan of economic cooperation and development for the Pacific island states is well and good. However, any such clear-cut formula, in the name of a comprehensive plan, without the enthusiastic participation of the recipient states will no doubt be perceived as tantamount to an imposition by the donors. A "Marshall Plan" may serve a very useful purpose if it is an exercise put into effect following an inflicted catastrophe and devastation as has been the case in the past. There is no such situation at present. What is called for presently, to precede a comprehensive plan, is a far more tedious exercise--the task of "getting to know one another" better with the desire to create a "feeling of oneness."

The distinguished citizens from the Pacific island states amply demonstrated at the discussions the paramount value they attach to growth (cooperation and development) that is congruent with traditional values. Charles Lepani brought out this salient fact quite clearly: "Land ownership and cultural solidarity are two of the key variables that play a major role in determining political and economic stability in the long term in Pacific island nations." In the midst of internal pressures to adjust adequately to new variables, external pressures are being brought to bear one after another on the independent Pacific island nations. These, stated Charles Lepani, "point to a scenario of uncertainty in the world today. Some of the uncertainties that threaten the political and economic stability in Pacific island states are due to difficulties faced by the major economies of the world." These include sluggish conditions caused by large budget deficits, large balance of payments deficits in some major industrialized economies and large surpluses in others, debtservicing problems of the more developed group of Third World economies, and protectionist policies by major world markets and governments.

The views expressed and the issues debated at the first session of the forum had a significant impact on the audience. The following three sessions very much revolved around the topics raised in the first session, so much so that the Forum Statement (Appendix F) fully reflected the pressures caused by trade and payments surpluses, deficits, protectionism, and servicing of debts.

Commodities and primary products

The deliberations at the first session, which started off slowly but gained enthusiastic participation as the discussion progressed, gave the impetus for digging deep into the topic of the second session, namely the "The Impact of Market Conditions and Institutional Arrangements on Commodities and Primary Products," a topic of significant relevance and serious concern to the peoples of the Pacific island nations. Their small size and relatively small populations do not welcome any serious capital investments for industrial outputs other than those that might be considered as feasible for partial processing, in most cases of primary products. Under such circumstances, primary produce and crops play the major role in any economic stability and sociopolitical activities. Understandably, any pressures on these will have an effect on how governments of independent Pacific island nations will react when external pressures are bought about without concern for the well-being of the peoples in their island states.

The first session with W. W. Rostow, Eni F. Hunkin Jr., Toru Yano, and Charles Lepani set the stage for the second by highlighting trade deficits and surpluses, their impact on market conditions, and the vulnerability of commodities and primary products on which smaller developing states were very much dependent. The subject of the second session proved to be far more significant to the Pacific island states than to the major world economic powers that had to deal with runaway deficits and surpluses.

The world sugar market and Fiji's sugar industry were eloquently described by Rasheed A. Ali. He pointed out how the interaction of forces of supply and demand for commodities could become distorted under a different set of market conditions to the severe disadvantage of developing nations that are "dependent on a narrow base of agricultural commodities."

Yasukichi Yasuba addressed the forum on the commodity problem with special reference to the South Pacific. He referred to the predictions of the Club of Rome, made about 16 years ago, that world food production would not meet the explosive population growth and that food prices would have to rise sharply. Small developing countries, with hardly any industrial base, set their economic policies toward the rapid development of food and agricultural products, not only to become self-sufficient in such commodities but also to earn foreign exchange through the export of such products to world markets and thereby meet the costs of other urgently required development programs. Ironically, the prices of all farm products started to decline in the 1970s. A case in point, as described by Ali, is the crucial state of Fiji's sugar industry, the life-line of Fiji's economy.

Peter Drysdale too in his paper on South Pacific trade and development assistance elaborated on how very dependent for their well-being the South Pacific countries are on primary commodity trade and foreign aid. All three speakers could not help but draw the attention of the participants to the fact that the price support policies adopted by industrial nations toward their own farm productions have put the efforts of the South Pacific in a state of severe turmoil. The encouragement and the aid poured in by international organizations and donor governments has turned out to be in fact a disillusionments because these organizations concentrated their efforts on improved and greater commodity productions and completely ignored a marketplace for such products. In the world marketplace, these small nations have little ability to sell their products at reasonable prices.

It has been common for industrialized and economically powerful nations to urge the aid and technology recipient developing states to perform better and to practice better work ethics. Such dictates appear to have dampened the enthusiasm and aspirations of the small developing nations and only increased their frustrations. This was amply demonstrated by Papilea Foliaki, a forum attendee, when she urged a temporary exchange of places. She suggestes for instance, sending the people of Tonga to live in a country that is highly developed economically and letting them push the high-tech buttons for a year while a similar group from the economically developed nation moves to Tonga and takes care of Tonga's primary produce. Undoubtedly, this was a worthwhile diversion for the participants engaged in heated discussions over commodity prices. It made the point clear to all: The nurturing of "oneness" in the midst of diversity among all inhabitants of the globe has to take precedence over all other matters. Perhaps this is what Foliaki had in mind.

The role of technology

The third session took up the topic of "Technology as a Transformational Resource," an appropriate and natural sequence to the previous two topics. Trade deficits and surpluses being experienced by the industrial powers, the mounting anxiety over commodity prices in the face of protectionism, and pressures on the primary products of dependent developing countries all appear to have a salient relationship to the economic, social, and cultural impact of technology on society.

The speakers for the third session were C. T. Maiden, Robert E. Driscoll, Tau'ili'ili Uili, and Kei Mori. The kind of technology that is to be introduced to a particular country has to be related not only to the educational attainment of that society but also to the social, cultural, and economic structure of that society. Maiden invited the attention of the participants to these issues when promoting the transfer of technology. In this context the development of educational facilities on a regional basis was highlighted. While this makes great economic sense, especially in island states within a region with small populations, it was pointed out that island states are proud of their traditional customs and cultural values and would be averse to any infiltration or dilution. There is no doubt that a happy medium has to be struck. Educators will have to pay careful attention to issues such as the length of academic or technical training most appropriate for a region, and periodic training to desired levels.

Maiden discussed these aspects during question time. It was clear that people were becoming increasingly aware of these types of concerns.

All assembled were in full agreement that the introduction of appropriate and/or new technologies did bring about significant economic growth. Some countries benefitted immensely while others did not take full advantage of this resource. Driscoll detailed how the assimilation of technology in the Asia-Pacific region has brought about significant exports of a large array of technology-intensive, sophisticated products. The creation of an environment for private, entrepreneurial initiative and government-industry cooperation for research and development has contributed to the success of technology assimilation.

While discussing the topic of technology as a transformational resource, Driscoll quite correctly touched on some of the problem areas as well. These were breaches in technical transfer agreements, such as infringements on trade names and marks, patent rights, wrongful disclosure of technical know-how to third parties, and similar nonprotection of intellectual property. It is no doubt very important that both parties should play their parts in safeguarding industrial property rights and know-how. It is equally important that recipients of a technology be made fully aware of their responsibilities and rights as well as mutual obligations. At later discussions, it was pointed out that quite often technology and know-how transfer agreements are written solely from the transferrer's terms and point of view and seldom in full consultation with the recipient. They also often do not take into consideration the socioeconomic and cultural background of the country. All in all, it was the general view that technology as a transformational resource has helped immensely in the dynamic economic growth of the Asia-Pacific region as a whole. With greater creativity in the assimilation process of new technologies and with the systematic transfer of appropriate technologies to areas that are just in the early stages of assimilation, the whole of the Asia-Pacific region could turn out to be an example for the rest of the world to adopt.

Appropriate technology

The next speaker, Tau'ili'ili Uili Meredith, drew serious attention to the role of technology from a South Pacific islander's perspective. He rightfully urged the forum to consider what is appropriate technology in an island setting. Very often what may be considered as the technology of the day may be totally inappropriate in an island state. He gave several striking examples of cases where technologies introduced in good faith by outsiders turned out to be utter failures, given the island setting and its living environment. In fact, some turned out to be health hazards.

Another important subject Uili touched on was the recent worldwide enthusiasm for biotechnology. With careful manipulation, biotechnology can be made to serve mankind better and improve the value and quality of agricultural products. However, one should not lose sight of the importance of and thus sacrifice the diversity of crops, and perhaps throw some into extinction, considering the fragility of island ecosystems. In warning of all the possible long-term ill effects that could result from short-sighted applications of biotechnology, he in a sense belittled the advantages of the science. Uili, however, welcomed its appropriate applications in agriculture, livestock, fisheries, and forestry on which most of the Pacific island states will continue to be dependent for a long time to come. Furthermore, he made a plea requesting the economically and industrially powerful countries to refrain from introducing technologies that could adversely affect fragile island ecosystems.

The Pacific island states have become custodians of vast sea areas in comparison to their small land mass holdings since the introduction of the new law of the sea regime. Both living and nonliving seabed resources do require higher technologies if they are to be properly managed and utilized. However, they must also remain as an important food resource to all the Pacific island states. Any depletion of these resources, whatever the causes may be, can be catastrophic. Thus the subject introduced by Mori, the marine ranch concept, which utilizes the bountiful solar energy in tropical waters for producing food for the fish and thus ready supplies of fish for people, was indeed a timely subject for all island states to consider. With very little land and few lakes or rivers, there is very little promise for aquaculture. Additionally, the cost of feed in fresh-water aquaculture together with inherent disease problems can become a major setback. In contrast, solar radiation is harnessed to cause the production of useful food organisms for fish that are managed in ranches. Open invitations were extended to Mori to set up such ranches. The concept of fish ranches was common knowledge to most island fishermen, since it has been practiced by them in the form of fish-attracting devices (FAD). Mori's new concept, however, is much more sophisticated and interested many.

Dealing with deficits and surpluses in major trade arenas, ensuring appropriate levels of prices for commodities, and assimilating or innovating technologies that are in harmony with ecosystems are a balancing feat. But who is responsible for balancing technology, primary produce, price levels, and so on? Of course it is humanity. Development of this balancing capability as a valuable resource is of paramount importance.

Human resources

The fourth session, "Development of Human Resources," was aptly dealt with by all the speakers. Resin Moses in his address repeatedly stressed the value that we must place in the individual and the need not to let that value decline simply because there are too many individuals. Once the value of any one individual is acknowledged, then the method adopted to develop human resources will undoubtedly change for the better. The impact of communication and information technology on the youth of the Pacific island states has been phenomenal in recent years. Should they be restrained from access to such world trends? Should they be compelled to hold on to historical traditions? These are questions that today's parents in the island states find difficult to answer. As a matter of fact such difficulties are not specific to island state parents, they are worldwide. How do we develop our valuable human resources so they are in harmony with world trends in technology, politics, economics, the arts, the sciences, and so on, and at the same time contribute maximally to the society in which the individual lives.

These questions were discussed in the paper submitted by Lau Taik Soon, which gave Singapore and its development of human resources as an example. He stressed the importance of education, training, and the continued refresher programs most appropriate for each field of activity. He maintained that the capacity and ability of each individual should be assessed and his capacity and ability be efficiently utilized. In this context, institutional responsibilities are indeed great in the training and development of human resources so as to provide the best labor force to meet specific needs. There is no denial of high standards of productivity. However, the method of developing such valuable human resources will inevitably have to vary with differing social and cultural systems and of course with changing patterns of civilization.

Several participants voiced their individual opinions on issues raised during the sessions. Saburo Okita called on all to appreciate the importance of the Global Community Forum as a venue for the free and frank exchange of opinions. The common conflicts of the North-South tension in the Pacific never surfaced and in contrast, aspirations to achieve viable developmental targets in a spirit of "oneness" were evident throughout the discussions. He stressed the importance for developing countries to maintain political solidarity and the increasing necessity for the world community to recognize different categories of countries that can benefit from and contribute to the world economy in different ways. In this context and in order to build a better and more viable world economic system, he categorized the major emerging economies, namely the newly industrialized countries and countries that are already close behind, as those would integrate themselves progressively into the market-oriented international economic system. For the less developed or poorer countries, the national entities of which are increasingly becoming a global issue, he maintained that it is of utmost necessity for industrialized countries to respond more positively to their specific developmental needs. Ignoring such needs could only aggravate the dependency of these nations, and if that happens then industrialized nations will have to blame themselves. The sharing of experiences will benefit all and ensure wholesome growth of the world community.

Though the situation in the South Pacific is entirely different from the devastated economic state that prevailed in Europe after World War II, a development plan with concepts somewhat parallel to those of the Marshall Plan was discussed by Kozmetsky. He mentioned that the Pacific islands have transformed themselves through their own efforts and have become important members of modern society. To lead themselves into the twenty-first century, a viable framework, a plan, worked out by the islanders themselves will be most useful. The plan should not be thrust upon them from outside but generated from within and actively supported by the world community, particularly the industrialized rich, such as the United States and Japan. George Kozmetsky also emphasized the importance of education and training, particularly in the fields of agriculture, and invited the dispatch of promising South Pacific students to his institution.

In the same tone, R. Gordon Jackson and Tupuola Efi both stressed a review of aid programs tailored to specific needs, enhanced regional trade, and world market access to commodities. Other speakers also mentioned their own country's experiences in the development process. With will and determination, it is possible for a country to jump from "stone-age" conditions to modern lifestyles in a matter of decades.

Need for communication

The Global Community Forum 1987 was special in another regard. Several who were not physically present were still able to participate in realtime via lunaphone technology and to give their views on global cooperation and the important role Asia and the Pacific have to play in future years. John D. Rockefeller, speaking from Washington, advocated the need for the United States to forge a healthy partnership with the Asian-Pacific region by identifying common interests, challenges, and responsibilities.

Michio Nagai, speaking from Tokyo, stressed the importance of cooperative efforts in all spheres of development. He further emphasized that unity amidst Pacific diversity had already been achieved to a great measure and that further mutual consultation and understanding would secure peace and prosperity for all.

Mohammad Sadli, speaking from Malaysia, related the growing feeling of mutual and combined understanding that has culminated in united actions for cooperation, such as the Association of Southeast Asian Nations (ASEAN). He was therefore very optimistic that the global forum would activate a similar consensus for a wider program of cooperation within the Asian-Pacific region for the collective good of all.

One of the prime initiators of the Global Community Forum was the late Ichiro Hattori. His sudden death just weeks before the 1987 forum was a shocking blow not only to the organizers of the 1987 forum, since he had participated in all the preparatory meetings of the organizing commitee, but also to all participants of the meeting. It was indeed an honor to all at the forum that Takako Hattori, his widow, attended the forum not only to fulfill her late husband's mission and dedication to the aspirations of the Global Community Forum but also to express her will and desire to contribute toward global cooperation and development. It was therefore fitting that at the opening of the sessions all participants observed a moment of silence in honor of the late Ichiro Hattori and also to say a deeply felt Thank you to Mrs. Hattori.

The man primarily instrumental in the success of Global Commuity Forum 1987 was Hiroshi Matsumoto, secretary general of the current forum and the two previous forums. His tireless enthusiasm was all-pervasive. All participants expressed their gratitude for his remarkable ability to look into every minor detail that contributed to generating a feeling of "oneness" throughout the conference. The chairman too should be congratulated for efficiently conducting all the sessions and for drawing up the forum statement to the full satisfaction of all the participants. The statement reflected the true concerns of the participants and particularly the deep concerns of the Pacific island states.

The greatest thanks go to the people of Western Samoa for the warm hospitality they extended and for playing host to the 1987 forum. From dignitaries to the man on the street, all Western Samoans desired that the forum should be meaningful. It achieved that goal. All participants became sulis ("heirs") to mother earth.

Keynote Address

Va'ai Kolone

I salute and beg forebearance of the sacredness of the Dawn at Tiafau!

Your forebearance--you, the chosen doves, from afar.

I salute--the collective dignity here gathered at Tiafau, ("Parliament House") the Malae, ("open space in the middle of a village") of Peace and Serenity!

I salute and recognize the height and depth of the wisdom and the philosophies of the four corners of this inhabited Earth

You, who have emerged together like the golden wild oranges of the Samoan cascades,

All hail, felicitations and salutations!

As in the Samoan expression, the ship that saileth has touched the city in mooring and the ship within the Chiefly House retains security.

Let us give thanks therefore to God the Omnipotent for the gift of life and good health!

May I greet you now in all your excellence and human dignity.

Honorables, excellencies, I warmly welcome you! Grace our House with your gracious presence.

Take your place--and may you be divinely inspired!

The full name of the ceremonial green upon which this Parliament stands is Tiafau, Le Malae o Faautugatagi a Samoa ("the place where the Parliament House is located").

Or the place where sighs and cries are muted and where tears of anxiety, injustice, and violence are removed.

Because it is at Tiafau that Power and authority decide for peace and justice unto whosoever is in need.

For this reason, I am deeply moved and gratified to witness this occasion, when the representatives and participants from the different parts of the world of the mind and the different concerns of mankind have come together to Tiafau, Le Malae o Faautugatagi, to confer, to consult, and to communicate on issues of mutual concern pertaining to the twenty-first century--which is but a pace away!

The twentieth century is a troubled and restless time, when nations are at war with one another. But it is also the century that has seen the unheard-of developments and marvels that the human mind can reach and can produce.

It is the century when mortals walked the moon and where outer space is as familiar to the scientist as the palm of the hand.

Yet it is also a time when the nations of the world seem unable to create peaceful relations with one another--an era where the emphases seem to underscore everything that divides.

But you have come together here at Tiafau. And my hope is steadfast, a hope for which everyone in this land--from His Highness the Head of State, Susuga i le Malietoa to the littlest Samoan--is observing the meditation of the Tapuaiga ("Act of worship"). My hope is that out of your deliberations and shared concerns a vision for world peace will be established, and man would once again wish to be valiant for friendship and be at peace with self and fellow man.

One other reason why I am very happy to greet you this morning is my personal belief that the Samoan philosophy of the faamatai ("to become or to do the way of matai") has relevance to the purpose of this distinguished gathering.

Samoan tradition and culture are founded on the philosophy of the faamatai. Each matai is chosen by the heirs of the particular matai title to serve, to protect, to develop and to be the refuge of his extended family.

The matai is the trustee of the aiga ("extended family") land and heritage; he is the keeper and protector of the family traditions and the champion of the aiga's rights. The matai's responsibility is to produce as much as possible to be shared evenly by as many of his aiga as possible, aiming always for peaceful relations within the aiga, village, district, and indeed the whole world.

The philosophy of the faamatai insists on consultation on all things. Consensus and unanimity are the goals--always.

The faamatai is careful of the safety and security of each member of the aiga; he is full of patience and tries to consider all issues with care and responsibility, because the aim in view is always peaceful consensus and unanimity among all heirs.

I firmly believe that the philosophy of the faamatai and its decisionmaking process is probably among the most difficult to implement and practice.

Nevertheless, my hope is still high, for one of the most difficult aspects of the faamatai has already been achieved by your presence this morning.

You, the matai and decision-makers of the different disciplines and spheres of human endeavors, have gathered here at Tiafau to talk together, to share our hopes and our visions--as equals and as responsible *international matai* who are aware of and concerned for the prosperity and peace of the twenty-first century--a future that you hold and we hold within our hands.

I wish to acknowledge our gratitude and sincere thanks to Mr. Hiroshi Matsumoto and the Association for Promotion of International Cooperation of Japan (APIC) for making our country the venue of this meeting. *Faafetai tele lave* ("Thank you very much").

Now, as Prime Minister of the first Pacific country to achieve political independence, I, Va'ai Kolone, with due respect and deep appreciation for this opportunity do declare open this third meeting of the Global Community Forum.

May the God and the Source of All that is Perfect, Just, and Peaceful be with you all in your deliberations.

Soifua ("Good-bye").

Part *I*

*Current Experience and
Future Potentials of
Economic Development in
the Pacific Region*

Chapter 1

A Challenge for the Pacific Basin

Walt W. Rostow

It is now more than 20 years since Kiyoshi Kojima first proposed an intergovernmental economic organization for the Pacific basin. Despite many thoughtful symposia, backed by learned and wise papers, such an organization has not yet come to life. As an Australian member of Parliament said to me in 1983: "When things have gone well, the governments asked, 'Why do we need a Pacific basin organization?' When there were crises, they were too distracted with immediate problems to think about it."

I have come here to Western Samoa from Austin, Texas, not only because I've never been able to refuse a request of George Kozmetsky but also because I believe a solution to a critically important international economic problem of our time would be substantially eased if we were to confront it in the first instance as a multilateral problem of the Pacific basin. I refer, of course, to the problem posed by the continued large U.S. balance of payments deficit and related Japanese surpluses. Major political and strategic as well as economic issues depend, for all of us, on when and how we make the inevitable adjustments to the present intolerable situation.

I gravely doubt that this problem can be solved by Japanese-U.S. bilateral negotiations alone. The solution requires deep changes in domestic policy in both countries, and in others as well. My central theme is that these domestic changes will be easier for governments to undertake if they are based on new multilaterally agreed rules of the game. In the end, such rules must be acceptable and accepted beyond the Pacific basin; but there are good reasons to begin here. And before I have finished, I shall propose a quite specific way to proceed.

First, a brief word on why it has been so difficult to set in motion an intergovernmental organization for the Pacific basin. The reason is that discussion began in the 1960s on analogy with organizations that had had some success in Europe or the Atlantic for example, the Common Market, the Free Trade Zone, and the Organization for Economic Cooperation and Development (OECD). These are all essentially organizations of advanced industrial countries. It has only gradually become clear that the art of organizing the Pacific basin is to create a setting in which countries of quite different stages of economic growth can work comfortably together. To be blunt and specific, we need an organization whereby the Association of Southeast Asian Nations (ASEAN) members, let alone the small Pacific islands, will not feel threatened by the weight of the United States and/or Japan. We shall see that this central point--the spectrum of stages of growth in the region--is highly relevant to defining new rules of the game for trade and payments.

Second, new rules of the game must be based on a clarification of how and why the international system worked in the century from 1815 to 1914 and, indeed, how it worked under the Bretton Woods agreements from, say, 1945 to 1971. Those relatively successful systems were not based on free trade as opposed to protection. The United States, for example, and some of the continental countries were notoriously protectionist before 1914; and the so-called scarce currency clause permitted discrimination against the dollar under Bretton Woods--an exception widely but not always wisely exploited. In the pre-1914 century, as many have emphasized, Britain's open capital market and post-1846 free trade were helpful. But the key to the success of the system was an unwritten agreement about domestic policy; namely, governments would accept the international transmission of business cycle depressions as well as periods of prosperity from the world economy to their domestic life. Bretton Woods was also based on assumed domestic rules of behavior--for example, exchange rates fixed in terms of the dollar and only formally and occasionally adjusted.

But in the end neither the United States nor other major partners in the system were willing to make the changes in domestic policy necessary to permit Bretton Woods to continue to work. We all took the easy way out with floating exchange rates, partly under the illusion, fostered by the macroeconomic textbooks, that relatively painless exchange rate adjustments would leave governments free to pursue domestic economic policies of their own choice without external discipline or penalty.

It can be--and often is--argued that floating exchange rates were the wisest--perhaps the only--policy we could pursue in the wake of the breakdown of Bretton Woods. There is something in that judgment. But, as a recent analysis has concluded, "floating exchange rates has applied no discipline on countries to pursue more compatible policies. And it has allowed misaligned exchange rates and unsustainable patterns of payments imbalances to build up."[1]

Putting aside all the technical complexities of the trade and payments problem, what we confront, in fact, is a set of unreconciled domestic political problems: U.S. and Japanese in the first instance but, also, problems for virtually every other government in the Pacific basin and, ultimately, of course, for the Federal Republic of Germany, the other countries of Western Europe, and for Canada as well.

This is not the occasion to provide detailed prescriptions. But, clearly, the United States must find a bipartisan political base for bringing the federal budget into balance, easing interest rates in order both to maintain a high rate of growth in the U.S. economy and to ease the debt problem of developing countries. In my somewhat unorthodox view, the United States should also be prepared for a period of strict incomes policy that would damp inflationary pressures and strengthen the U.S. export position without excessive further depreciation of the dollar. There are, in addition, longer run measures relating to the generation and, especially, diffusion of new technologies that ought to be undertaken. All of these measures require not only a political bipartisan consensus but business-labor cooperation of a kind going forward at the state and local, but not yet at the national, level.

As for Japan, the Maekawa Reports have set out better than any non-Japanese analysis or prescription the profound reorientation and rebalancing of Japanese life away from an obsession with maximizing its balance of payments surplus, toward more diversified domestic and foreign policy objectives that are required if Japan is to become what it must be--a critically important guarantor of a new international system that once again links domestic policy to the viability of the world economy.

But responsibility does not end with the United States and Japan. Growth in the rest of the world has come to depend on increases in exports to the United States financed by a buildup of U.S. debt that is simply not sustainable. Let me cite a few statistics. In the period 1981-1986, the United States experienced a cumulative merchandise trade deficit of $593 billion with a cumulative interest and investment income surplus of about $150 billion. A recent calculation indicates that even if the United States were to bring its trade account into balance as early as 1992, it would have to borrow an additional $560 billion to cover its cumulative deficit over the period 1987-1992 plus its interest and investment income deficit.[2] Clearly, not only Japan but all of the countries of the Pacific basin will have to reduce their reliance on earning surpluses in trade with the United States and look elsewhere for sources of effective demand.

We are talking, then, about a restructuring of trade in the Pacific basin and throughout the world.

The fact is, of course, that neither the United States nor Japan has made anything like adequate progress in these directions. The devaluation of the dollar promises some but quite inadequate relief in the next several years;[3] the U.S. international debt position is building up in an intolerable way, and no effective leadership is being exercised to head off a major crisis. Frustrated by the stalemate between the president and the Congress on the federal budget, and by the failure of the Venice meeting to yield decisive movement by Japan and the Federal Republic of Germany, the protectionist sentiment in the U.S. Congress is likely to continue to gain momentum.

In those circumstances, how could collective action by the countries of the Pacific basin help? The answer is that there is a decent chance, at least, that the political balance in both Japan and the United States might be tipped favorably by a process set in motion by three actions. First, a strong multilateral statement of the vital collective interest of the Pacific basin community in an orderly resolution of the trade imbalance problem in ways that avoid three real dangers: a global recession, a surge of protectionism, and the exacerbation of the debt problem in the developing regions. Second, a general statement in support for rules of the game that, while recognizing the differing responsibilities of countries at different stages of growth, would apply to all members of the community. Third, the suggested appointment of a small wisemen's group, of the kind that helped solve key problems in Europe on several occasions in the 1950s and 1960s, to propose concrete rules of the game.

There are firm foundations for a procedure of this kind rooted in authentic interests and needs. Every country in the Pacific basin would gain if the trade imbalance is solved properly; every one will lose if it is not. The Pacific basin--indeed, the world economy--is characterized by a progressive diffusion of power. No single country can lead as Britain did in the half century after 1815 and the United States, in the quarter century of Bretton Woods. Responsibility must be shared not only between Japan and the United States but also between the intermediate economies of the region, including the emerging new industrial nations. Finally, new rules of the game do require definition, for none of us can any longer be under the illusion that a regime of flexible exchange rates permits each nation to safely manage its economy as short-run convenience and domestic politics dicate.

I do not believe, as do some of my colleagues, that a return to the gold standard makes sense. For one thing, it worked in its day only because citizens were prepared to accept the rigors of recurrent deep depressions. And, attractive as automatic mechanisms may appear to be, there is no turning the clock back. On the other hand, we cannot manage the world economy without creating a consensus on responsibilities we bear in our domestic dispositions for the economic health of the community as a whole.

Finally, I believe it will be easier for both Japanese and U.S. politicians to do what needs doing if they are acting--and are seen to be acting--in response to objectively defined communal principles rather than to bilateral pressures of one kind or another. For we should be quite clear: the Pacific basin may not yet have yielded a viable intergovernmental organization, but it is a powerful idea of great attraction. When I came through the region in 1983, talking with many private groups and officials of twelve governments, we talked candidly of the difficulties that had to be overcome if an organization was to emerge for the Pacific basin. But I found also that a sense of community already existed--a sense of the region's great common destiny--and a judgment that, in time, it was inevitable that the governments organize to work together.

Even now I am confident that if the community could find its voice on the complex issue of trade adjustment, that voice would have a benign and significant influence.

I would not pretend to foreshadow what a group of the Pacific community's wise men might agree on, but in broad terms the necessary headings are clear enough.[4]

- Agreement that large persistent surpluses and deficits are inconsistent with the health of the region and the world economy when allowances are made for capital-importing economies at an early stage of growth, economies in the process of reducing abnormal indebtedness, and other specified exceptional circumstances.
- Agreement that all members of the community will act in ways to reduce disruptive surpluses and deficits on a rather short timetable.
- Agreement that such actions be taken with two further objectives in mind: to maintain growth rates and, in light of still unresolved debt problems, to keep interest rates low.
- Agreement to cooperate in making the necessary structural adjustments--a provision required because the elimination of the U.S. trade deficit will inevitably reduce the possibilities of building growth in the Pacific basin on the basis of expansion of exports to the United States at previous rates. This problem heightens the importance of the commitment to make the necessary trade adjustments in an environment of rapid expansion in the world economy.
- Agreement to set up a regular trade- and payments-monitoring mechanism for the Pacific basin, not merely to oversee the execution

of the new agreed rules of the game but also to prevent the buildup of inappropriate surpluses and deficits in the future.

Under present circumstances, of course, our wise men would have to be quite specific in their recommendations for action by the United States and Japan under some such principles.

I should, perhaps, underline that the proposal I am making here today reverses a stance on a Pacific basin organization I have taken on other occasions.[5] I have argued that it would perhaps be wise to move slowly and gradually, demonstrating, step by step, that an intergovernmental organization would do initially modest but useful things. Thus I welcomed the proposal of Indonesia on July 12, 1984, at the historic Six Plus Five Pacific basin session in the wake of the ASEAN meeting in Jakarta. That proposal was for concerted work on human resource development, a subject that would generate urgency and high-level interest if it were focused on human resource requirements for absorbing efficiently the new technologies, for technology transfer has always been and remains overwhelmingly a matter of trained men and women. And I have added other items to a possible working agenda,[6] for example, multilateral examination of future innovations stemming from the current technological revolution; systematic examination of future resource and environmental requirements, with special initial emphasis on reforestation; and intensive studies of the problems of and possibilities for development of the small Pacific islands, many of which represent severe challenges to the theory and practice of economic development.

Why, then, should I now propose as an urgent multilateral intergovernmental task this difficult, complex, and sensitive matter of the trade imbalances and their resolution? The answer is the one suggested at the beginning. Progress is dangerously slow; the scale of U.S. indebtedness is mounting to unsustainable levels; and a convulsive nationalist reaction by the United States could endanger the economic, political, and strategic viability of the Pacific community. The issue is too great to be left to the narrow domestic politics of the United States and Japan. The voice of the Pacific community should be heard and heard soon. In the wake of a successful outcome, the Pacific basin could go on to organize itself on a wider, long-run agenda. But the long-run will not be very promising unless our governments unite to cope with our immediate problems in good style.

Notes

1.   Val Koromzay, John Llewellyn, and Stephen Potter, "The Rise and Fall of the Dollar: Some Explanations, Consequences and Lessons," *Economic Journal* 97: 385 (March 1987), 34.

2. These estimates are from a paper by Richard Drobnick and Selwyn Enser, "Pacific Rim Trade Scenarios: 1987-1992," originally prepared for a research workshop held on April 2-4, 1987, sponsored by the International Business Education and Research Program of the Graduate School of Business Administration, University of Southern California.

3. See, notably, Ralph C. Bryant and Gerald Holtham, "The External Deficit: Why? Where Next? What Next? What Remedy?" The *Brookings Review* (Spring 1987), especially 31-32. This report on an international workshop on the prospects and remedies for the U.S. balance of payments deficit exhibits the projections of five well-known econometric models. They all predict some resumed worsening in the U.S. balance after limited improvement in 1987-1988.

4. For a somewhat similar, but not identical, set of broad criteria for global rules of the game, see Bryant and Holtham, *The External Deficit,* 35.

5. See, for example, *The United States and the Regional Organization of Asia and the Pacific, 1965-1985,* (Austin: University of Texas Press, 1986), especially 95-130.

6. See, for example, *ADB Quarterly Review*, QR-3-85, (July 1985), 9, for the agenda I proposed in Tsukuba, Japan, at Expo '85, in May 1985.

Chapter 2

Japan as a Civilization

Toru Yano

Japan's international friction

Friction between civilizations

One thing that may readily be discerned from the relations between the United States and Japan in the last several years is the fact that friction between the two nations is about to be taken for granted. Moreover, Japan finds itself in a position in which it always sustains "bashing" from the United States. Furthermore, the "bashing" itself may become notably radical on the basis of unilateralism. The beginning of a coordinated intervention in the appreciated yen and the depreciated dollar by the Group of Five, representing the finance ministers and central bank governors of five industrialized countries, in May 1985 did not dramatize or signify what is called "Japan bashing" here. But the latest retaliatory measures against Japanese semiconductor imports have appeared as part of a serious pattern of Japan bashing, which could be taken as a reminder of the United States' possible posture toward Japan in the future.

Not only are the relations between the United States and Japan deteriorating, but the friction between Western Europe and Japan is taking on a serious character. In Japan's relations with Britain, a new dispute has flared up on cable and wireless access to the Japanese market, to say nothing of Britain's rapidly rising trade deficit with Japan and Japan's tariffs on imported British whisky. In Japan's relations with continental Europe, the European Economic Commission's recent decision to impose "antidumping tariffs" on Japanese imports has given rise to serious psychological friction between Western Europe and Japan. Japanese semiconductors are being examined by the Common Market from the perspective of possible dumping violations.

It is suspected universally among West European nations that Japan alone might take the lion's share of the game if it is played according to the common rule of free marketing. Nevertheless, as long as free market principles cannot be discarded, out-and-out procedural restrictions or moral restrictions in line with the theory of an "equilibrium of interests" might be worked out one by one against Japan. When it comes to the question of grim prospects, the relations between Western Europe and Japan are in no way an exception.

Some people argue that another war has already broken out between Japan, on the one hand, and the United States and Western Europe on the other. But those proponents are urged to exercise more prudence in using the word "war." It is not true that the United States and Japan are in a state of war. In fact, I am getting along well with many friends and acquaintances in the United States, and I know many of them still have a fancy for home electric appliances and autos of Japanese manufacture. There remains no change whatever in the need for getting a hold on reality in relations between the United States and Japan.

This may be said not only of relations between the United States and Japan but also of those between Western Europe and Japan. But when we take a look at only those areas in which friction takes place, we find a serious state of affairs. When we take a look at these areas where there is no friction, however, it might be said that the relations between Western Europe and Japan are really friendly and good. Friction of this sort has many points of similarity to what astronomers term "collisions in space." Even if galaxies collide with each other, the distance between stars is too far for them to crash into each other. But there is no need to say here that collision does take place in an extremely dramatic way once in a while.

With this in mind, let us think of the motif of "friction between civilizations." Historically, there have been many instances in which two heterogenous civilizations meet, giving rise to a wide variety of conditions. The latest instance has surfaced in the form of friction between the United States and Japan and between Western Europe and Japan. The premise is that Japan, per se, has its own civilization. Later, I shall go into detail about this point. There is little doubt that relations between the United States and Japan and between Western Europe and Japan are moving toward a dimension that cannot be explained away using theories on economic or cultural friction, or toward a dimension in which they could essentially crash into each other. Nevertheless, this friction should *not be construed as a war in any sense.*

The friction between civilizations, as referred to here, has a number of features.

One is that as long as two civilizations are in contact with each other, there emerges an aspect by which both try to insert their own civilization's characteristics into one another's world. With the dissemination of elements of American civilization in Japanese society, which results in the process of being "Americanized," the Japanese lifestyle permeates deeply into American society. Paradoxically, such a peaceful dynamic is a fundamental feature of the friction between civilizations.

A second feature is associated with high technology vis-a-vis friction. A fine example is the stiff relations between the United States and Japan in the high-tech sector of semiconductors. As long as civilization remains as it is, competition arises because there exists a subtle difference in ability. In this context, the friction between nations may be likened to the emulation that occurs among honor students. In the political and economic sectors, moreover, the guiding fundamentals and rules that are unique to the citizen-oriented modern society remain intact, and there emerges an aspect of friction that is totally heterogeneous compared to a pattern of friction between the civilized and the not civilized countries.

A third feature is that the friction between civilizations is never transient. The friction is perpetual in nature; it almost chronically sustains inself in such a manner that a dispute over a civilizational factor A may be followed by another over B. Besides, no solution satisfactory to both sides is in sight.

Fourth, the friction between civilizations, while serving to deter the exercise of sovereignty in the ultimate form of a war, leads to one between governments with the exercise of sovereignty in other forms. Nevertheless, as we have seen earlier, it is normal that peaceful and civilized relations are mutually sustained and that the mutual assessment is basically high. In other words, in the same way that people are equipped with intelligence and the latitude with which they may be able to look at sources of friction with presence of mind, so, too, do we see examples of discretion in the public sector that attempt to resolve friction between parties involved as far as possible. However, this is not the case in the private sector.

In fact, the United States and Japan are not crashing into each other as imperialist countries are wont to do, to use Leninist jargon. In essence, it is more appropriate to describe the United States and Japan as being actively involved in the process of learning. It is correct to perceive that both nations are in the process of evolving the logic of an international order in which mutual interdependence will result in closer relations in the future. No precarious signs at all are visible, such as the possibility of an imperialist war breaking out in the long run as a result of an ongoing scramble for markets.

Japan's historical cycle

The exchange rate is to rise to 140 yen to the dollar, but nobody believes that it will stop there. This is quite an unusual phenomen, albeit predicted. There are strong signs that the United States, not satisfied with efforts for a strong yen, might go in for mutualism or protectionist measures. The friction between the American and Japanese civilizations is likely to become all the more severe.

Efforts for an appreciated yen and a depreciated dollar in the last days of September 1985 proved to be a major turning point for Japanese history. The year 1945, forty years earlier, was another major turning point. It is hardly necessary to add an explanation here, as it is well known to all that that year witnessed a disruption in Japanese history in the form of Japan's defeat. In this regard, the turning point of history in 1985 was so subtle that it cannot be perceived without deep insight.

Japanese history seems to have evolved in major cycles of 40 years. Forty years before the year of Japan's defeat, in 1905, the Russo-Japanese War came to an end. Even the amateur student of history is aware that that year was a major turning point in Japanese history. And forty years before 1905 was the Meiji Restoration.

For teaching the history of diplomacy, the Russo-Japanese War provides a great impetus. It was not so simple a war, and even though Japan won it, there was much reflection on many aspects of the war. Therefore, Japan had many problems after the war had come to an end.

Out of this reflection came the concept of accelerating nationalization of the railways. During the Russo-Japanese War, most of the Japanese railways were private. There were many private railway companies across the nation, and it was procedurally difficult to transport cargo during the war. In 1906, a bill for the nationalization of railways was forced through by the Diet, providing for the purchase of railways by the government.

The history of the Japanese National Railways (Kokutetsu) is said to have been 115 years in duration, but I have the strong impression that it was an 81-year period. The word *Kokutetsu* strongly implies that the destiny of the nation was to be shouldered by Kokutetsu. This implication arises because Kokutetsu was substantially borne out of the circumstances that followed the end of the Russo-Japanese War. All conceivable meausres were taken to beef up the national strength or the war potential. The founding of the Japanese National Railways was one of those strategic considerations. In this context, it seems more reasonable to count the history of the Japanese National Railways from 1906, the thirty-ninth year of the Meiji era. Incidentally, it was also in 1906 that the Manchurian incident occurred.

The period of nearly forty years from the Meiji Restoration to the Russo-Japanese War was indubitably a period of civilization and enlightenment. Even though the essentials of its political dynamics remain ambiguous, it incorporated the restoration as a vehicle for the revival and strengthening of the emperor's civilization in which attempts were made to create "pseudomorphosis," at least in the superficial sense. In those years, Japan was immune to all sense of shame in modeling itself after the West.

During the forty-year period from the Russo-Japanese War to Japan's defeat in World War II in 1945, Japan, which had become more or less civilized and enlightened, dared to demonstrate to the world whatever it had learned in a high-handed system of power balance. Eventually, Japan was beaten to a pulp after it had unreasonably opted for an agreement with Germany and Italy against communism.

The forty-year postwar period was, as we have already seen, a period in which a new experiment in civilization was being conducted. But "the flow of civilization" is not the product of a deliberate strategy; it has developed spontaneously. In Japan today, there is neither political nor economic awareness, and there is a lack of awareness about civilization.

I do not mean to say that I would take such a cycle of forty years for granted, but I am compelled to feel that the year 1985 was a year of disruption in history. Furthermore, I would not term developments in 1985 anything like those of the "1985 revolution," but it is true that the objective environment that surrounded Japan changed dramatically enough to warrant that expression. The appreciated yen that will not embark on a reverse course in the future was one of the signs. The "deadlocking" of the heavyweight industries, to say nothing of the privatization of the Japanese National Railways, has similar characteristics in the sense of a liquidation of past history.

If that is the picture, it would be advisable to look ahead and begin grappling with unknown historical conditions, instead of dreaming of a reversion to Japan before 1985. Personally, I am in favor of this posture. In other words, the period of forty years from 1985 to 2025 is an entirely new cycle of history, and our task ought to be to strive to develop prospects for the long-term period of forty years.

This is something anybody can foresee, but the Japanese people will probably drink from the bitter cup of life from now on. This next forty-year period that will contain many hardships has just started. If things are left as they are, what will become of Japan?

Japan will doubtless be forced to pay the price of civilization in many ways. Domestically, the reorganization of the economic structure will be in progress and serious questions will be posed one after another in relation to measures for Japan's national land. There will be no end to the hypertrophy of Tokyo and the National Capital Sphere. Conversely, the depopulation of each local region will leave "progress" in a state of morbidity. Even though the Fourth Comprehensive National Development Program is underway, there will be rapid progress in the degeneration of Hokkaido and Kyushu, providing further indications of the difficulties to be faced in the coming forty-year period. As regards Tokyo's hypertrophy, however, it is noted that its debilitation will move into a phase where there will emerge factors undesirable for Tokyo, giving rise to minus factors that could be termed the "Tokyo question." As is discernible from the historical precedents of every civilization, many distortions will emerge in society and the alienation caused by civilization among human beings will give rise to a wide variety of unfortunate dramas, unless political fundamentals and rules are strictly abided by.

Externally, the Japanese civilization will steadily proliferate as a lifestyle kind of civilization, spontaneously creating what might be called a Japanese sphere, or a sphere over which Japanization extends. Whether such a Japanese sphere is to be developed as a national policy is entirely another matter, but the prerequisite seems to be for us to intelligently prepare ourselves for how this proliferation of civilization will evolve and what sorts of problems, or what sorts of friction in civilization or culture, it will produce in each region of the world.

The people who are conscious of the "Japanese sphere" may be classified into a "global group" that takes it for granted that the Japanese mode of living will spread across the world without regard to regions and an "Asian group" that projects that the sphere will be formed in a concentrated fashion in Japan's peripheral area. It is historically corroborated that Japan, whose economy has steadily grown, has put "spindle effects" (to use the words of Miyohei Shinohara) on its periphery and helped the nations that have retained relations of interdependence with Japan develop according to the logic of the Japanese type of development. The area over which the "spindle effects" have extended might be called the "Japanese sphere," but as far as Japan's strategy is concerned, it would be reasonable to grope for spots or social spheres where dialogue is reasonably feasible.

The fact that the Japanese economy has developed with a high degree of dependence on foreign trade tends to be called to account, but in another aspect, the fact remains that the assessment of and taste for Japanese products are on the rise and not on the decline. At least in the sectors of those products in which Japan specializes, its relatively superior international competitiveness will be retained for the time being. Moreover, insofar as Japan's merchandise exports are concerned, prudent and optimistic views might be considered more realistic than pessimism.

One feature of Japan's postwar foreign trade lies in the fact that it has successfully converted the average Japanese citizen's lifestyle into a system of exportable merchandise. This is a considerably significant point. Japanese consumers are never represented by the rich but consist of wage earners whose wage levels are even and for whom the space of residence is limited. This very fact has brought about a significant impact on the input of noneconomic values in the merchandise production process.

It might be argued that this feature has enabled Japanese merchandise to have an increasingly deep significance and relationship in terms of values with global buyers, with the result that the global base of the Japanese merchandise market has become all the more secure.

Japanese exports, which have evolved around an exportable everyday-life mode, serve to create a kind of unique lifestyle sphere in the periphery, precisely because they have evolved around the spindle of an across-the-board system of life modes. Buyers in the People's Republic of China and Southeast Asia find more familiarity with Japanese products than those of Western manufacture. The criticisms of the inundation of Japanese products are ironically a barometer of the general populace's strong taste for Japanese products.

This fact per se suggests a danger for Japan. The challenge from Europe and the United States will persist. The appreciated yen and the retaliatory measures against Japanese semiconductor imports among others are only the first step. Diplomatically, there could be numerous measures with that to bash a Japan that tends to keep to itself. Then there are all kinds of demagogy to slur the image of Japan. In the last decades, the "question of the Soviet Union," or the question of communism, has been in debate as it is tied with legitimacy and heterodoxy within the European continent. From now on, however, I am compelled to feel that another grave question for the European community--the argument for the Yellow Peril or the question of the Far East's paganism--will at least psychologically come to fore.

In any event, Japan will be burdened by serious friction between itself and other civilizations in the next thirty or forty years. The conditions will be of a kind never experienced by any other country and may well go far beyond what one might imagine.

A state with one paradigm of cultural values may not be compatible with a state operating under other paradigms. For example, the national paradigm of the United States that hypothesizes a state as an open system has characteristics far different from those of a paradigm of a Japanese type. It is inevitable that such national paradigms clash with each other once in a that, for the state functions as a mechanism of civilization. In the framework of civilization, the state is something that should be secondarily positioned as a functional device. As long as the state asserts its absoluteness, civilization will not remain the way it naturally ought to be.

In this regard, there are many factors on which we ought to reflect. One is that among the industrialized Western countries, Japan is conspicuously nationalistic. Or it would be more advisable to say that Japan has within itself characteristics of the kind to drive its counterparts at the negotiating table to take a nationalistic posture. At least, the recognition that Japan is strengthening its nationalistic posture is widespread throughout the world. The *Far Eastern Economic Review,* a leading weekly magazine in Asia, came out with a cover story on Japanese nationalism, and even *The New York Times* featured articles on the subject in one of its Sunday editions in April 1987.

Tragically, Japan is always held accountable for the transformation of the conditions in which essentially refined and civilized nations meet each other, that deteriorate into irrational relationships. The foundation of Japan's tragedy is sustained by its unique bureaucracy.

Japan's scenario

There is no doubt that Japan is involved in civilizational friction with the West. The danger in this circumstance is for Japan to come out with one nationalistic response after another and try to cope with the situation merely with mercantilism, from an economic perspective alone. For example, if attempts are made to handle the situation only by focusing on the appreciated yen and attempts are made by businesses to locate points of production in foreign countries and internationalize the purchases of parts and components, the situation will not be rectified to any great extent.

One relief from friction between civilizations is that the relief lasts over a time span of 30, 40, 100, or 200 years. In other words, Japan has the free scope to think, even though it finds itself involved in really severe friction. Instead of merely conceiving the situation as economic or cultural friction, there is a need to learn the basic differences between the West and Japan in a wide variety of aspects, such as law, administration, education, the sense of the state, the comprehensive spiritual structure that encompasses the values of man, nature and society, as well as models of art. Then what should Japan take into account? For the moment, I wish to enumerate the following four points.

First, Japan should make continued efforts to develop her image as a civilizationed nation. Globally, there is confusion about the image of Japan. The strong image of Japan with an inherent culture remains intact, on the one hand. On the other, Japan is visualized as an ambivalent country that is not cultural and has nothing to do with civilization. Then there has recently emerged a new image of Japan that has created a new type of civilization. The mention of *Europe* brings to mind a civilization of dazzling beauty, while the term *Japan* is not associated with an image of the values of civilization--at times--Japan is even associated with a barbarian image.

In order to build Japan's civilizational values, the national sense, the sense of institution, and the sense of legislation ought to be mature. Besides, more effort has to be undertaken to come up with a "universal language" in the sectors of thought, ideals, philosophy, and art. In particular, there is a need to establish an academic tradition of distinctive character that is full of originality in the sectors of science and technology. In all these spheres, Japan still does things by halves.

Second, various aspects peculiar to *kanchi kokka* ("country governed initiatively by bureaucrats") have to be internationalized to eliminate the friction of civilization. There is a need to convert the government machinery into a learning system that is full of international sensitivity. The motif of the government as a learning system did exist in the early years of the Meiji era. Surprisingly, it has disappeared in recent years, and there are strong signs that Japan leans toward the principle of precedence and the principle of abidance by domestic law. It is necessary that the so-called administrative reform should not only aim at simplifying the administrative machinery but should be oriented toward the creation of a learning ability and a self-reforming ability within the administrative machinery.

The third task is grappling with the new frontier and the burden of its cost. In the future civilization, there will be calls for sincerity toward foreign countries. Japan must show its sincerity in dealing with "world problematics," such as the North-South question. Japan must mobilize intelligence in defining the "world problematics" of its own accord. It is indeed significant for Japan to strive to retain the center of international intelligence in the sense that it will play such a function.

In particular, Japan's technological level is high. Moreover, the appreciated yen turns out to be a kind of bonus for Japan. Given those factors, Japan could extend dynamic economic cooperation in the development of the Third World. Japan has a really broad range of possibilities, from steady humanistic contributions by nongovernmental organizations to large-scale experiments in the engineering of civilization, and the main area to which Japan could contribute is Asia. To grapple with the development of Asian countries with sincerity will be the test case for Japan for the time being.

Fourth, on the premise that the force to sustain civilization in the future is neither armed force nor formidable economic power as in the past, but the ability to deal with information in a broad context, Japan must develop a perception with which to consider comprehensive "wisdom" as a force and look for a method to equip itself with this force. The predisposition of Japan, which is better at reception than transmission, is rather a virtue, but it should be an option befitting Japan in terms of civilization to brush up its transmitting ability to a conspiciously greater extent than its receiving ability. In this regard, it is to be noted that Japan is burdened with a national research system that does not befit a civilized nation, as is deducible from the present absurd system of examinations for admission to universities. We should take serious account of the necessity for building Japan into a nation that lives on information by balancing software and hardware. An information-oriented society predominantly composed of hardware is not suited to the sustenance of civilization. There ought to be "global wisdom" in a more generous context.

With the enumeration of the above four tasks, there is nothing specific to add to my essay on the friction between civilizations. Starting with a debate on sanctions against Japan on semiconductors, my presentation of issues might have evolved in a roundabout manner. In a nutshell, it will by no means help to solve problems in the relations between the United States and Japan and between Western Europe and Japan by alternating hope and fear whenever difficulties arise. What Japan is in need of is a constitutional reform of the state. For this, a perspective drawn from the theories of civilization is required.

If Japan does not change itself at this time, then it would fail to overcome the friction between civilizations and will eventually be forced into a state of isolation. One dreadful outcome from friction between civilizations is that if a given temporal and spiritual latitude is not used to develop an effective response, then Japan will sustain a fatal retaliation. The ultimate retaliation has yet to come. Japan must take serious account of this point.

Asia-Pacific region and Japan

The Asian Development Bank as a symbol

The Asian Development Bank was formally founded on November 24, 1966. It was the very year in which the Americanization of the war in Vietnam became increasingly conspicuous. It was the year in which the Great Proletarian Cultural Revolution got under way. It was also the year in which Suharto came to power in Indonesia.

In Japan, it was the year in which the national population exceeded 100 million, a decision was made for the construction of additional facilities at Sanrizuka for Tokyo International Airport at Narita, and Nissan Motor absorbed Prince Motors. In a nutshell, it was the year when there emerged signs of a sort of "fetal" movement for what Japan's future would look like. That year, Japan and other Asian nations, were attempting to grope by trial and error for a new future scenario, as they had nothing definite in their future.

Given the tendencies at that time, the newly founded Asian Development Bank was to play a symbolic role in many senses and it was only natural that this regional bank should do so. Given circumstances in which all was unsteady and in a state of flux, there was every reason to believe that an institution whose *raison d'etre* for being established was clear, should play a symbolic role for the future's sake.

More than anything else, it is to be noted that the Asian Development Bank was established as a symbol of Japan's foreign policy stance to establish new relations with the rest of Asia, while striving to depart from the traditional posture of alienating itself from Asia and turning toward Europe. On the surface, the founding of the Asian Development Bank was based on a decision made by the United Nations' Economic Commission for Asia and the Far East (ECAFE), but the fact of the matter was that Japan took the initiative in giving birth to this bank and in fact became the primary investor.

To this move on the part of Japan, other Asian nations responded with contradictory feelings of expectation and apprehension about Japan. Eventually, they came to accept Japan's part in Asia and its ability to contribute to the rest of Asia.

The framework of the Asian Development Bank is so designed that Japan is supposed to have an "indirect" part in Asia. There is no need to point out that this experiment has been crowned with glittering success. At a time when direct involvement does not necessarily prove successful in the end, the *raison d'etre* of this bank is indeed of significance in the sense that it has demonstrated the importance of contributions in the form of indirect involvement, granted that the contributions might not directly add to an exaltation of Japan's prestige.

"Family doctor" theory. At or around the time of its establishment, the Asian Development Bank was likened to a "family doctor." In plain language, this meant that the bank was intent on becoming an institution like the neighborhood family doctor who treats people with a cold or stomachache. This perception itself is really of Japan's own making in every sense of the word. It was, indeed, a reasonable option for Japan in dealing with the Asian region, which was in a state of disorder without a competent core of power for unification and where a wide variety of local troubles cropped up.

The stance in which attempts were made to give life to Asia's own characteristics with attention riveted on potentials in the tropical agriculture of this region, the productivity of which is higher than that of any other region of the world, by grappling with not only the development of agriculture but that of industry as well, might be described as the right option when attempts are made to launch international financing activities in the Asian setting.

The basic policy line of the Asian Development Bank remained wholly legitimate when the People's Republic of China put its Four Modernizations on the right track and Japan decisively established its position as a major economic power after the war in Vietnam was brought to an end. The form that Japan's economic cooperation with the rest of Asia ought to assume in the future can be easily deduced from this fact. For another thing, it must not be overlooked that the Asian Development Bank has turned out to be an important lever not only for Japan's policy but for that of the United States as well.

The United States, which markedly lost interest in Asia after its fiasco in the Vietnam war, still continues to have a strong interest in this region with a view to sustaining its initiative. This is discernible from its stand of investing as much in the Asian Development Bank as Japan does. This also seems to be deduced from the United States' policy to curb Japan's special additional investment as much as possible, which would be tied in with a revision of the share of the voting rights.

Indeed, the question of Japan's special additional capital outlay is symbolically significant in the sense that it will determine the degree to which the United States can have a say in the Asia-Pacific region.

In any event, it is evident that the Asian Development Bank is a versatile symbol of the problems and roles in the Asia-Pacific region, and the history of the Asian Development Bank fully symbolizes the regional development of Aisa.

Design for Asia's regional development

In the last 20 years since the founding of the Asian Development Bank, Asia has made conspicuous progress on the whole. In the meantime, there have been critical moments, such as the oil crises, and Asian countries in general have made steady progress and developed regional economic features of their own in an unstable global economy.

Basically, this uniqueness may be observed first in the relations of functional interdependence that evolved around Japan's "axial effects" (to use the words of Miyohei Shinohara). On the basis of Japan's axial effects, Taiwan, the Republic of Korea, and other newly industrializing countries have increasingly and positively made inroads into the global market, and ASEAN member nations have also been able to make steady progress in labor-intensive sectors. Having said that, it might be stressed that the whole of Asia has now moved into an entirely new situation, something unprecedented in world history.

Unique regional economic features. First, a unique scenario of decolonization began in Asian countries. In the last 20 years, the Asian economy has extricated itself from the monocultural legacies of European colonial rule and has entered a phase of industrialization. The fact that many countries have ceased to depend on their suzerains and have come to have closer ties with Japan exemplifies the fact that this region is entering a new phase of history. For them, the European way of life is now a remote one.

In addition, the adherence to monoculture that characterized the colonial rule, or the vertical division of labor, has collapsed, and the level at which nations develop has reached a point of sophisticated industrialization that may well be tied in with the building of an exporting capability.

Second, the North-South problem in this region has taken on a unique character. The structure of economic interdependence that has presented itself in this region involves a process in which the industrial production capacity of industrially developed countries is relocated in the region in an effective manner, so much so that the North-South problem, that normally brings to mind the image of an intense confrontation between both sides, has instead been marked by mild confrontation.

Naturally, against the background of this superficial impression, the North-South problem, that is essentially international in nature, is responsible for the appearance of serious economic contradictions within each country. In this context, it must be said that the "international alleviation" of a series of issues associated with the North-South problem goes side by side with the "domestication of economic contradictions." In any event, it is worthy of note that the North-South problem in the Asian region is significantly different from the one that is normally visualized in the rest of the Third World.

Third, in this regard, I would like to point to the question of "incomplete graduation." By every standard, Taiwan, the Republic of Korea, and other newly industrializing countries in Asia can no longer be categorized as belonging to the South. Judging merely from the fact that their gross national product and income levels are striking, and that they are raising their shares in the world's industrial product market, these nations can well be described as countries of the North.

By stopping the horizontal division of labor in the sector of industrial products, these newly industrializing countries have alleviated the North-South problem for themselves and have come to a point of "graduation" as they have cast aside their qualifications as countries of the South. Nevertheless, these countries' consistent position is to avoid "graduation," in principle. There are a number of psychological factors that encourage this posture. As is discernible from the vexations held by the South Koreans toward the Japanese, that posture is tied in with feelings of the kind that take root in history and have nothing to do with economic rationality. The economic activities of these nations will go on to the point where their "graduation" has to be accepted as a consequence. There is no doubt that they will cast light on the unique North-South problem of this region.

Fourth, the economic development of this region makes it inevitable for it to associate itself with the United States as a merchandise market, thus crystalizing the question of what is known as the "Pacific rim." An important point of this concept is illustrated by the fact that the idea of the Pacific rim is formulated and advocated as an international issue not by the United States, but by Asia, centering on Japan. In actuality, however, the conspicuous merchandise exporting capacity of East Asian nations has resulted in exposing the weaknesses of the U.S. economy and, ironically, in giving rise to serious trade friction.

As one of the desirable theoretical experiments of economic interdependence, the concept of the Pacific rim holds the promise of an important future, and there is undeniably the possibility that it might seem offensive to the United States, which has to confine itself to resource industries, such as agricultural production and oil, or the exceedingly sophisticated industries in which high technology is put to full use. In this context, the latest friction over trade between the United States and Japan is serious indeed.

In the process of such economic maturity of the Asian type, there is no need to point out that the Asian Development Bank has played an effective

Bright and dark sides of interdependence

In spite of such maturity on the whole, there remain many issues that have yet to be solved in the Asian region. If it is assumed that the questions posed to this region are those that evolve around an adjustment of relations between nations in conjunction with the region's deepening interdependence, many questions that are associated with the peculiar interdependence of this region will come to light.

Basically, the magnitude of the lag between the political interdependence among nations and their economic interdependence must be taken up as an issue.

The disruption of relations between nations that should be termed an after-effect of the cold war remains an unfortunate reality, as is the case with the situation of the Korean peninsula. An unusual global interest is focused on the Seoul Summer Olympics scheduled for 1988, whereas there are no signs at all of a thaw in relations between Vietnam and the People's Republic of China.

In contrast, Asia's economic interdependence is growingly substantially. Judging from bilateral relations, multilateral relations, relations within the region and relations between the Asian and other regions, this region is rife with moves toward increasing economic interdependence. Naturally, it cannot be said that there are not smuggling and other evils, but the

Asia-Pacific network of economic interdependence is sound and creates economic relations that can well stand up to a reasonable analysis.

In the future, this region's interdependence will depart from the mere flow of merchandise and money and begin to function in the flow of information and service. And the flow of people, as is represented by immigrants, will increase with the wage differential as an incentive, if it is left as it is, and might fill up the gap in the labor cost between nations. As regards the flow of people, it is to be noted that the migration of a massive labor force is a matter that calls for sophisticated political judgment. In this sense, the flow of a labor force will take on an aspect in which the deepening of interdependence is slowest.

Having said that, what will make the economic interdependence substantial in the future will be direct and indirect investment by the private sector and international financing. Direct investment might be an inevitable option for Japan, which is faced with the strong yen. For a similar reason, Japan's indirect investment will also be on the upswing. With the advent of an era of off-shore markets, Hong Kong, Singapore and other Asian cities will stand side by side with Tokyo as powerful pivots of international financing, and there will emerge a new form of network interdependence.

With this development, the industrially developed countries that center on Japan, while seeking a relative mitigation of the national framework, will strive to develop a new system of globalism, or a systematic framework of economic interdependence, whereas developing countries, while striving to strengthen "public nationalism" (to use the words of Hugh Seton-Watson), will attempt to develop and strengthen their national economies.

Herein lie factors for the appearance of subtle distortions in perception between nations within the Asian region. In no way must it be overlooked that there remain signs of the expectation of national creativity within the Asian region.

As is discernible from many precedents, even socialist countries that assume a resistant attitude toward political interdependence will grapple positively with the formation of a framework for economic interdependence. In such a situation, however, there are many cases in which effective relations of economic interdependence can hardly be materialized. Because of the way in which a national economy is established, because its practices are different, and particularly because no private business is available, the qualitative delineation tends to become a barrier.

A good example is the People's Republic of China today, which is fighting against difficult odds in its attempts to achieve the Four Modernizations. The system of national institutions has a direct bearing on the success or failure of economic interdependence. In this context, the transformation of political conditions and the deepening of economic interdependence do not necessarily make for proportional progress. Insofar as economic development is concerned, the question of national institutions is extremely serious.

Lack of interdependence in ASEAN region. The Asian region is strikingly multifarious in terms of the distribution of economic capabilities, including the availability of resources, so that Asian nations supplement one another.

Nevertheless, there are limits on interdependence with resources. The relations tend to be unchanged in which the countries that export primary products are always the countries that offer resources, whereas industrialized countries import cheap primary products and live on exports with values. Cases in point are Indonesia, whose economic growth is unsteady even though it has oil, and Malaysia, which is threatened by drops in the prices of primary products. Interdependence in this context would not function in an effective manner. It is to be noted that reciprocal interdependence of the kind that encourages the normal development of each country is a desirable form of economic interdependence.

With regard to Southeast Asia, there are signs that the deepening of interdependence among ASEAN nations is considerably slower than their cooperation with nations outside the ASEAN region. In cooperation with the ASEAN region, the zero-sum pattern hardly dissipates, and where similarities in the economic structure function as minus factors and what is of benefit to one country are not necessarily so to another.

Another feature is the imbalance between surplus market forces and industrial productivity. There seem to be hardly any ready solutions to the dilemmas, such as in the case of Singapore, which has a high production capacity but is limited as a merchandise market, and of Indonesia, which has a broad frontier for the marketing of merchandise but is inferior in the production capacity.

Given these conditions, there is hardly any willingness to revitalize the economies within the ASEAN region by taking effective advantage of this economic dependence. To escape this dilemma, it may be necessary to work for a bold diversification of production items and to raise the possibility of organically combining the economic features of each country. For this, the essential thing will be the extent to which the social "modernization" of each country is to become qualitatively flexible and substantial.

Japan's task

Be that as it may, the economic interdependence of this region will increasingly deepen, with a wide variety of issues possibly coming to the fore. Nevertheless, the deepening of interdependence does not necessarily result in giving birth to a peaceful and reciprocal international order. Rather, the deepening of interdependence normally entails intricate competition and intense friction.

Moreover, more than anything else, the probability is high that whereas the interdependence of the Asian region will lend to parity in positions between nations, the structure of the vertical order, on top of which Japan is situated, will become solid. Social upheavals in each country will conspicuously go on with a wide variety of distortions, such as urbanization and the disruption of traditions, and unstable conditions of a kind that surpasses all imagination may develop.

In any event, Japan's future task must be to systematize measures of its own to cope with the region's deepening interdependence. Moreover, the climate that surrounds Japan will become all the more harsh. Indubitedly, Japan has now come to a point where it ought to develop a new philosophy of interdependence.

The Asian Development Bank, which was established in 1966, was, as it were, a cornerstone that Japan placed with prudence in an unstable Asia. In general, the future prospects of Japan and other Asian nations cannot be termed rosy. That is why it is high time for Japan to place another cornerstone with prudence, pondering the way that it will associate itself with the rest of Asia in the years to come.

Symbolically, Japan was forced to change its basic policy in trade relations with other countries in 1986, which marked the twentieth anniversary of the founding of the Asian Development Bank. In the midst of an incessant and rapid appreciation of the yen against the dollar that started at the meeting of the Group of 5 in September 1985, there have emerged drastic changes in the Japanese perspective on Asia. Greater changes are observed in economic relations between Japan and the rest of Asia.

The dependence of the rest of Asia on Japan will increase as it always has. In proportion, as industrialization progresses in newly industrializing countries, there will be an inevitable increase in their imports of intermediate or capital goods from Japan. Given the appreciated yen, there are growing signs that Japan will want to locate business entities and production pivots in foreign countries. The merits and demerits of this venture aside, Japan's presence in the rest of Asia will be all the more keenly felt.

On the other hand, Asian countries will place increasingly high expectations on Japan as an import market. Cries for greater access to the Japanese market might turn into a concerted movement within and without the Asian region.

And, more than anything else, it is important that there are signs of a shift among Taiwan, South Korea, and other newly industrializing countries to act in concert with Japan by counting it as a country rife with experience that serves as a precedent, instead of counting it as a rival. In this subtle context, the responsibility Japan assumes to the rest of Asia will become all the graver.

Scenario of internationalization. Countries in Asia fear lest Japan, trapped as a result of the rising yen, should do whatever it thinks it should in its national interest without caring how it looks. And they are afraid that Japan might strategically opt for a kind of "Japanization" with a view to beefing up its influence over the rest of Asia in an organizational context. While deepening the degree to which they rely on Japan, Asian countries will continue to be vexed toward Japan for its political indecision.

Japan ought to opt for an advance along the direction in which Asian nations may be organically associated with one another by groping for and sustaining the factors in the region that can stand up to a rational analysis or dialogue. It is to be recalled that the policy the Asian Development Bank has sustained in the last 20 years is similarly one that is designed to encourage rationality. Nevertheless, whether Japan per se can behave itself as a nation with rationality has yet to be seen. And for the Japanese, defining what is legitimately rational in the Asian community is a task that has yet to be accomplished.

In association with this task, the scenario of Japan's so-called internationalization is of significance. In defining what is the strategy for internationalization, it is to be noted that a perception focused solely on Japan's national interest would turn out to be a barrier to a desirable form of internationalization. Internationalization must be designed not only to shift Japanese society into a more readily accessible system but to build a peaceful and reciprocal international order around Japan. The argument for internationalization must not be confined to that of how Japan ought to be, but must be broadened to encompass an international vision in which particular attention is paid to the security and development of Asia.

In this context, Japan's future task basically calls for intelligent responses. I would think that there are calls for profound insights into the *raison d'etre* of Asia and changes in this region. Be that as it may, Japan has to change.

Chapter 3

Potential Determinants of the Role of the Pacific Islands Region in the International Economy of the Twenty-First Century

Charles Lepani

Introduction

For the purposes of setting the tone of our discussions in respect to this particular topic, I will briefly discuss several aspects of current issues relating to regional characteristics of the Pacific islands. These are some of the potential determinants in my view of the role of the region in the international economy of the twenty-first century. As one of the key determinants, the relationship between sociocultural systems and the colonial history of the island nations and dependencies will be relevant here. The resilience of culture through the land tenure systems and a kinship network based on reciprocal rights and obligations should form the basis of the Pacific islands' continued efforts in the development process into the twenty-first century. On the other hand, colonial history has had a profound impact on the lives of the peoples of the Pacific and continuously challenges the sociocultural systems creating an environment for change.

This paper will also examine briefly the implications of the event of political independence in the Pacific region. The 1980s is witnessing a review of the role of government, and Pacific island governments are themselves involved in this process of reviewing their own roles owing to pressures from the international economy to utilize resources efficiently. These pressures are brought about by problems of balance of payments, budget deficits, debt-servicing, and increasing protectionist pressures on international trade.

Last, the paper will raise questions of regional security and its consequences on international relations for the Pacific island governments.

Culture and colonial history

The Pacific island peoples are of mixed Asian, Melanesian, and Polynesian stock, and their culture and ethnicity reflect this mixture. Recent colonial history has added a new and more profound impact to the lives of the Pacific islanders. The history of this relationship continues to play a major role in shaping and influencing the nature of national development endeavors and international relations.

It would not be a useful exercise for the purposes of the forum to itemize and discuss what each variable is in the equation of sociocultural dimensions on the one hand and the influences of recent colonial history on the other. Nevertheless, some of the more salient variables in this equation need to be highlighted.

Land ownership and *cultural solidarity* are two of the key variables that play a major role in determining political and economic stability in the long term in Pacific island nations. At the same time, a study of colonial history often leads to a discussion of political and economic variables espoused by advocates of the dependency theory. Proponents of growth argue that it confers benefits of development to developing countries owing to the inflow of capital and technological know-how from the international economy.

Pacific governments remain appendages of governments of metropolitan administering authority, normally a division of foreign affairs or foreign offices, or long after independence, a separate ministry of territories. Development objectives and management of the economy reflect decisions relevant to economies of the administering authorities. The development and structure of the economy is necessarily linked to such decisions.

It is necessary to reflect on such a historical overview to explain reasons for public sector predominance in Pacific island states and consequent development objectives, strategies, and policies that were adopted by the countries at independence. The transitional stage before and after independence sees a dominance of donor multilateral agencies in their influence on policies to restructure the economies to achieve such goals and objectives.

Critical to the transition stage and political independence is the shift in the responsibilities and powers of financing development. The design of fiscal and monetary policies to enhance that effort toward self-reliance becomes an immediate concern of policy makers. Rarely, however, do governments in promulgating policy changes concern themselves with institutional reforms that must accompany fiscal and monetary policy changes to realize and implement development policies. The heavy and visible hand of governments becomes entrenched, consolidated, and expanded through objectives variously called economic nationalism, state capitalism, and redistribution of benefits of development to indigenous people.

The situation then becomes a big hand of the public sector with fingers in state enterprise established to foster indigenous business, government participation in major resource projects, government business ventures into production, distribution-marketing of goods and services that with careful decision making may reveal other instruments of policy as more efficient in achieving similar policy objectives.

Political independence

The event of political independence marked the beginning of a new reality for Pacific island nations. It meant that they may carry in their own foreign policies in determining with whom to establish economic and political relations. It allowed a quickening of the pace for and a broadening of the scope of dependency to the international economy and its political network. Control of the power to make policies for domestic social and economic development issues meant that labor force training and management skills became critical areas of concern for these newly formed governments. The role of the public sector became consolidated and often expanded after independence.

The changing role of the public sector in the 1980s

The governments of Pacific island countries face critical challenges in designing, implementing, and managing strategies, policies, and programs of development into the twenty-first century. Key policy decisions need to be made in their efforts to transform the structure of their economies and thereby improve and diversify their resource bases. They require resources that are often provided conditionally.

In the island nations, there are several common features and characteristics of the social and economic systems that need to be stated at this stage. First, the public sector is the largest single employer and its activities (expenditures) constitute a significant portion of the gross domestic product of the economies.

Second, the "rural" agricultural sector with cash and subsistence components have managed to sustain and provide for the livelihood of over 80 percent of the peoples of the Pacific islands. The cash component of the primary sector (inclusive of fisheries and forestry) remains dependent on international markets and the vagaries of commodity price fluctuations and increasingly protectionist policies of metropolitan governments.

Third, the Pacific island countries have a substantially young population, roughly over 60 percent of them with the working age of 15-35. Associated with this demographic characteristic is that the rates of growth have generally been high until censuses in the 1980s, which show some evidence of slowing down. Furthermore, the Pacific island countries are experiencing movement of people from "rural" to urban and from national boundaries to other countries.

Fourth, the land tenure systems combined with the extended family relationships based on reciprocity play a dominant role in the lives of the Pacific islanders.

The recent declaration of Economic Enterprise Zones have added a major dimension to the island nations' pool of resources and considerations of exploitation and management of them.

Last, the island states depend largely on capital flows of aid investment and international trade for their development. A significant policy consideration is the balancing of development trends and directions between externally sourced capital flows and domestic resources. The role of the public sector in setting appropriate policies for domestic and foreign resource mobilization and management will determine the long-term stability of the economies and their relations with the international community. Policy decisions on how much government intervention and where in the economy such intervention should occur will become increasingly important. Regionally, island states could be regarded as firms competing to sell similar primary products and facing similar cost structures. They are also competing for similar inputs, mainly donor aid funds, trade partners and investment sources should specialization occur in production as new resources are available. Regional forces become critical in the coordination of the process.

Earlier, mention was made of cultural solidarity and land tenure systems. Under different political systems, Japan and the People's Republic of China have depended on cultural solidarity to mobilize their resources to gain structural transformation in their economies. It is possible for Pacific island nations with their land tenure systems, a social fabric based on reciprocal rights and obligations, to offer policy makers options in domestic resource mobilization and their efficient application for development. There are a few cases that may serve to further illustrate this point.

First, subsistence production has provided for basic needs of food, shelter, and clothing for the majority of island people in the face of pressure to transform land and labor into production for cash. Second, in those countries of the Pacific region where outmigration of people to metropolitan and industrialized countries is possible through mutual intergovernment agreements, remittances from earned income in host countries to the home country are increasingly becoming a major component of the overseas payments side of the balance of payments accounts. These remittances contribute to improved per capita income of relatives at home.

The significance of the resilience of these manifestations of cultural solidarity is that government expenditure figures continually show minimal welfare payments from public funds. Furthermore, foreign-sourced capital assistance and investment should be used to augment the already self-sustaining base of production and income-generation capacity and should not allow such assistance to replace this base. Pressure is increasingly felt by Pacific island governments to efficiently manage foreign flows of assistance in aid (bilateral and multilateral), trade, and investment and at the same time to dig deeper into their domestic sources of capital and manpower resources to sustain and develop their economies.

This pressure is owing to difficulties faced by major economies of the world. Sluggish conditions caused by large budget deficits, large balance of payments deficits in some major industrialized economies and large surpluses in others, debt-servicing problems of the more developed group of the Third World economies (which only five years or so ago held the promise of booming economic performances because of to their natural resources), and protectionist policies of major world markets and their governments all point to a scenario of uncertainty in the world today. Such conditions will largely determine how the Pacific islands region will develop over the next decade.

The role of the public sector in the Pacific island economies in setting appropriate policies for domestic and foreign resource mobilization, application, and management becomes even more critical. At the same time, it should not continue blindly making comprehensive five-year economic plans and thereby allowing itself the license to intervene at all levels and sectors of the economies. Clearly, present day international conditions and changes in domestic resources and their use require a review of the role of the public sector. Appropriate monetary, fiscal, and regulatory policies need to be developed as well as budgetary and planning mechanisms to allocate resources and implement policies. The burden of development is a shared one.

Pacific island leaders meeting at Rarotonga in 1985 called for a program of research to assess the role of the private sector in the Pacific region with the main objective of reviewing key policies of fiscal, monetary, and regulatory controls and the necessary incentives to allow the private sector to assume a greater burden of development from the public sector. Shifting boundaries from the public to the private sector does not necessarily imply the public sector's abrogation of its responsibilities in overseeing that the general market mechanism operates efficiently in resource allocation. The success in shifting the boundaries of economic activity, particularly from public to private sector, and the response of the private sector to this overture by governments of Pacific island nations relate to the rest of the world in the twenty-first century. The cooperation and collaboration that need to be developed between the two sectors will be critical to the stability and prosperity of the region.

Security and resources ownership

In recent years security matters have thrust the Pacific islands region into the glare of the international community. Domestic political instability in certain areas, border problems in others, independence struggles, and the emergence of superpower rivalry are all ingredients that may contribute to the destabilization of the region and threaten its security.

A key consideration is that the Pacific islands region remains the last frontier in resources exploitation and development. For instance, the EEZs, as they apply to the nations of the region, mean that a potentially substantial pool of energy, mineral, and fishery resources of the world is controlled and owned by a relatively disparate group of island countries. They, in turn, depend on the technology, capital, and management know-how of developed nations to develop the resources. There is growing realization (particularly at this stage of sluggish real demand to generate production and employment in industrialized economies) that the Pacific Islands region has the potential to assume a greater role as a supplier of raw materials resources as well as provide markets for products of the industrialized countries.

Conclusion

This discussion has canvassed some of the potentially key issues that may force the region to play a more dominant role in international security issues and economic relations in the coming century.

The realization that the public sector itself cannot bear the burden of development is a positive step. Traditional or customary resources need to be utilized and developed in conjunction with outside assistance. Due care needs to be taken that regulation or moves toward privatization of public institutions, for instance, are not to the detriment of society. Efficiency should be the objective in public intervention or privatization. There are areas in the economy that require public or social intervention when the market has failed or is not the best alternative for the production of certain public goods or services.

In the long run, flexibility in public policy, given the unstable international economic conditions, will contribute greatly to stability in the domestic economic and political environment of the region. In turn, this will enable the Pacific island countries to play a more dominant and effective role on the international scene.

Chapter 4

Some Observations on the Present and Future Potentials of Economic Development in the Pacific Region

Faleomavaega Eni F. Hunkin, Jr.

Someone once said, "Please, dear God, make my words today sweet and tender, for tomorrow I may have to eat them." I recall an occasion upon which the world-famous tusitala ("teller of tales") Robert Louis Stevenson, complained of a bad habit the Samoans had of cutting off heads of their fallen victims in time of battle or while engaged in warfare. This was complicated by the fact that these same Samoans would be carrying their Bibles to church to learn more about their newly adopted Christian God and all there is to know about heaven and eternal life. The noted author later regretted criticizing the Samoans for this ancient practice after a prominent Samoan chief showed him a passage in the Bible, in which a young shepherd boy David killed the mighty Goliath with a sling-shot, and when he cut off Goliath's head with Goliath's own sword, God did not seem to mind at all.

Four years ago, Prime Minister Nakasone of Japan made a very interesting observation concerning world history and general movements of civilizations from one continent to the other. He said:

"History teaches us that civilizations shift gradually toward the periphery, creating new civilizations as they move. Flourishing civilizations have constantly moved towards the frontier; from Greece to Rome, from Rome to England, France and Germany, and from Europe to the American Colonies. Even within America itself, the torch of civilization advanced westward from the Atlantic to the shores of the Pacific Ocean. The compass needle of history has swung from the Mediterranean to Atlantic civilizations. Now it is pointing towards the Pacific. Today, there cannot be doubt that we are on the verge of a new economic and cultural sphere, that, while centered on Japan and the United States, will encompass the Pacific shores on both the northern and southern hemispheres. The Pacific Ocean is becoming the new and historic stage for the drama of human interaction and development. . . ."[1]

And rightly so, when one considers the fact that the Pacific basin alone accounts for approximately 60 percent of the world's gross national product. Furthermore, by 1990, approximately 62 percent of the world's population will be living in the Pacific. Since 1985, the United States has conducted at least a U.S. $185 billion trade and economic relationship with the Pacific, which is at least 35 percent more than its usual trade with Europe and elsewhere. Even the defense industry of the United States now depends on East Asia for major components of military equipment and hardware.

We recognize the fact that such statistics are quite impressive when the Pacific basin is taken into consideration, but we all know that such advancements in technology and trade are centered primarily in East Asia and not in Oceania with of course, the exception of New Zealand and Australia in this geographical area.

I would like to focus my remarks primarily on Pacific island countries and territories. These island nations and territories are situated in a geographical area commonly referred to as Oceania, and it includes all of Melanesia, Micronesia, and Polynesia. Basically, Oceania covers an area that totals approximately 7 million square kilometers, of which 70 percent is ocean. The region has a total population of about 5 million people, who speak over 700 languages and dialects, and is comprised of more than 1,300 islands and atolls. The region also imports annually in excess of U.S. $3-billion worth of goods and services primarily from Australia, New Zealand, Japan, Taiwan, Korea, Europe, and the United States.

As a Pacific Islander, I am in total agreement with a recent editorial of the *Pacific Island Monthly Magazine* (August 1985) which states, in part, that

> Seminars, workshops, discussion groups, and information exchanges are all very well for those doing the discussing and the exchanging. All too infrequently, however, are the people under a study present at these august gatherings. . . . The region (Oceania) has had just about all the "co-ordinating" it can take. . . Indeed, Pacific Islanders may well be the most studied people around today. . . . First it was the missionaries, then the explorers and the businessmen/opportunity seekers. Now, however, it's the age of the researcher. The procession through the islands of anthropologists, sociologists, nutritionists, economists, and whateverists seems never-ending. . . .Research opens up avenues for yet more research. . . .But the problems facing the islands are generally well-known and understood. No amount of studying or coordinating is going to solve them. . . And if the money spent on research over the years had been

invested in indigenous industries, there would be no need for all the research and all the aid.

The question that comes to mind is whether our region can make a difference economically and strategically in the overall equation of the world's socioeconomic needs, and the present ideological, economic, and military rivalry that now exists between the two super powers, namely, the United States and the Soviet Union.

Like many of you here this morning, I live in the middle of the Pacific Ocean with strong family ties and roots that are inseparably linked to an island culture that has had its existence for over 2,000 years. I cannot help but be concerned with certain economic and political events that have dramatically reshaped the region and its relationship with other countries of the world. Consider the following changes or trends that have occurred in the region only within the past eight years.

- The island territories of the Solomons, Tuvalu (Ellice Group), Kiribati (Gilbert Group), and Vanuatu (New Hebrides) have since become independent sovereign states.
- Serious confrontations have occurred between island countries and U.S. tuna vessels fishing within their 200-mile exclusive economic zones. The United States, however, has recently concluded a multilateral fishing agreement with 16 island countries. The proposed agreement provides for an annual cash grant of U.S. $8 million to be divided among the 14 island countries for a five-year period, and an additional U.S. $2 million in technical assistance for the Forum Fisheries Agency. Additionally, U.S. tuna boats will pay an annual license fee of U.S. $1.75 million and a U.S. $250,000-grant to assist island fishermen. The proposed treaty is now pending approval by the United States Senate.
- New Zealand stands firm in its present policy to deny all U.S. nuclear-powered warships and nuclear weapons access to its port facilities. As a result, the United States no longer shares any of its military secrets with New Zealand, and the Anzus Security Alliance is now seriously compromised.
- Besides having a full diplomatic relationship with Cuba, Vanuatu has recently decided to also establish diplomatic ties with Libya, the Soviet Union, and the United States.
- Kiribati now has diplomatic ties with the People's Republic of China, and in 1985 successfully negotiated a one-year $1.7 million fishing agreement with the Soviet Union. It is uncertain whether the agreement will be renewed between the two countries, but one may note that Kiribati is situated just about opposite of Moscow on the globe, and there is tremendous potential for future Soviet global communications.

- The South Pacific Forum countries last year established a South Pacific Nuclear Free Zone Treaty, which basically calls for the prohibition of any further purchasing, manufacturing, testing, or positioning of nuclear weapons in the region. The treaty, however, permits the transit movement of nuclear-powered ships and nuclear warheads within the region, leaving port accessibility to the discretion of the island states. The proposed treaty also calls upon the five nuclear powers, that is, the United Kingdom, the People's Republic of China, France, the Soviet Union, and the United States, to pledge themselves not to conduct any further nuclear tests in the region, and never to use or threaten to use nuclear weapons against any state within the area. To date, the Soviet Union and the People's Republic of China are the only major powers that have agreed to sign the treaty. Recently, the United States publicly announced its unwillingness to sign the treaty.

- For the past several years, practically all the Pacific island countries, including New Zealand and Australia, have filed protests before the United Nations and other forums against France for conducting nuclear tests in French Polynesia. To date, France continues to ignore the protests and nuclear testings are still in evidence in French Polynesia. The primary concerns among Pacific island countries are the possible hazards of consuming contaminated fish and other marine life since the nuclear tests are conducted underwater and the possiblity exists of radioactive fallout through the atmosphere.

- We now have three additional political entities in the region in the commonwealth of the Northern Mariana Islands, the Federated States of Micronesia, and the Republic of the Marshall Islands in free association with the United States. It is anticipated that the United States will provide approximately U.S. $2.2 billion in economic assistance to the above groups for the next fifteen years. The situation with Belau still remains uncertain.

- Fiji became the first Pacific island nation to successfully negotiate a U.S. $1.5-million bilateral aid agreement with the United States, in view of Fiji's strong support of U.S. policies in the United Nations and its dominance as the most developed island country in the region. Recently, however, Fiji was entertaining the possibility of negotiating a fishing agreement with the Soviet Union, and also of allowing Soviet ships the use of its port facilities.

- The original inhabitants of the French territory of New Caledonia--commonly referred to as Kanaks--in recent years have now asserted themselves against French colonial rule and are demanding either greater self-government or independence from France in the near future. New Caledonia is the world's third largest producer of nickel, and there are no indications that France intends to leave the territory.

- Calling themselves the "Melanesian Spearhead," the island nations of Papua New Guinea, Vanuatu, and the Solomons have held meetings to discuss regional needs and have also requested the United Nations to place New Caledonia for consideration by the UN Decolonization Committee of 24 and that the territory be administered by the Trusteeship Council of the United Nations.
- The presence of the Soviet Union in the Pacific Basin is now very much a reality--militarily, politically, and economically.

It is my understanding that last year Gorbachev spent more time on Asia-Pacific than on Europe. It should also be noted that of the Soviet Union's four naval fleets, the largest operates in the Pacific with approximately 400 ships, with over 100 submarines. The Soviet Union also has some 50 divisions of land forces strategically situated in East Asia. Note also that one-third of Soviet intermediate range ballistic missile forces are located in East Asia. And with its present utilization of Cam Rahn Bay in South Vietnam, Admiral James Lyons, commander of the United States Naval Pacific Fleet, commented that the Soviet Union now "can cover all the important sea lines of communication through the South China Sea, Strait of Malacca, and the eastern part of the Indian Ocean. And from Cam Rahn Bay, they can certainly launch strikes anywhere in Australia. . ." This is also true for East Asia and the Pacific.

After being apprised of the above trends and occurrences in the region, how does one go about formulating a comprehensive policy to meet the economic needs of Pacific island nations and territories? In my opinion, it would be unrealistic for us to discuss economic development and cooperation between the region and the industrialized countries without first understanding and appreciating the diversity of cultures, languages, and sociopolitical developments in existence in the Pacific today.

Our region has had experiences with the ravages of war and colonialism. But it has never had a Marshall Plan offered for greater economic development. I suggest that the industrialized countries of the Pacific Basin *collectively* formulate a Marshall Plan to provide economic assistance to the region for real development with the basic infrastructure--better schools, roads, harbors, health services, electricity, and water. No doubt, there has been tremendous goodwill and understanding between the region and the industrialized nations of the Pacific. Japan, Australia, New Zealand, Korea, and the United States have all contributed substantially to the economic needs of the region, athough all have different reasons for doing so.

It is common knowledge that the primary thrust of U.S. involvement in the region is and will always be strategic interests of national security. It should be noted that our region is situated right in the middle of all the most important air and sea transportation routes between the United States and East Asia. It appears, however, that there has been a slight shift in U.S. foreign policy in the region, as indicated several months ago by the remarks made on

September 29, 1986, by the new assistant secretary of state for East Asian and Pacific affairs, Gaston Sigur. The following are some highlights of his remarks:

> Today, the implications of daily events in Asia and the Pacific are truly global. . . .We cannot afford to regard the area casually as we deliberate our labor policies, trade strategies, or security provisions. . . .In support of our many defense commitments, we seek to maintain the overall strategic balance among major powers in the region which ensures our own operational ability, maneuverability, and access in time of crisis. . . .We will play a significant role in bringing appropriate technology to the Pacific to improve the job market and living standards of the area's people. . . .Very recently, within the past three or four years, the Soviet Union has demonstrated virtually unprecedented interest in the Pacific states. They have sent their emissaries to explore commercial and diplomatic opportunities in the area. . . .For our part, we do not view the Soviet initiatives in the South Pacific with particular alarm or distress. We do, however, sense the importance of preventing the areas' conversion into yet another area of major power confrontations. . . .The emergence of the Pacific as an important regional and even global actor is one of the great phenomena of the 1980s. (U.S. Department of State, Current Policy no. 871.)

Someone once said that the problem with diplomatic rhetoric and pronouncements is that officials never really mean what they say. What are some of the implications of Sigur's policy statements? Is he suggesting that the United States can no longer afford to take a passive role in the region? Must the United States continue to rely primarily on New Zealand and Australia for direction on matters affecting the economic and political stability of the region? What kind of technology was he referring to that the United States should bring to the region?

It is very likely that nothing much will occur to cause a major shift in U.S. foreign policies in the region until after the 1988 presidential elections. It is questionable for a change of policy even after a newly elected president takes office, since policymakers in Washington are still planning and fighting World War II in Europe despite the tremendous surge of trade and economic development that the Pacific and Asia have experienced with the United States for the past twenty years.

It would be well for the United States to increase its economic assistance programs to meet the growing demands of small island countries. The region, as yet, is not asking for guns or military hardware, but for serious developments in roads, hospitals, agroindustries, education, and trade skills to improve its economic standing with the rest of the world community.

Any leanings of island countries towards Marxist-Leninist philosophy is a direct result of the Western democratic countries' willful neglect and their inability to understand and appreciate the islands' economic needs. The United States cannot expect to pursue an aggressive and strong strategic military presence in the Pacific and at the same time fail to provide for the economic needs of the region. The only option available to these countries is to turn elsewhere for economic assistance, and it may well be the Soviet Union--as is now the case in certain areas of the region.

Selected Bibliography

Alves, Dora, "The South Pacific Islands: New Focus Needed for U.S. Policy," Asian Studies Center, Heritage Foundation no. 34 (August 28, 1985).

Ashbrook, Tom, "U.S. Faces Challenge in Pacific," *The Boston Globe*, (September 29, 1986).

Australian Foreign Affairs Record, "South Pacific Nuclear Free Treaty Bill 1986," Vol. 57, No. 7 (July 1986).

Craven, Steven, International Trade Administration, U.S. Department of Commerce, "Notes on U.S. Commercial Policy for the Pacific Islands," (May 31, 1985).

Crossette, Barbara, "Papua New Guinea and the 20th Century," *Honolulu Star-Bulletin*, (November 14, 1986).

Dalrymple, F. Rawdon, "The Pacific at a Turning Point," World Affairs Council, San Francisco (February 18, 1986).

Derwinski, Edward, Statement Before the House Foreign Affairs Sub-Committee on East Asian and Pacific Affairs, (September 10, 1986).

Dorrance, John C., "Oceania and the United States - An Analysis of U.S. Interests and Policy in the South Pacific," National Defense University, Washington, D.C. (June 1980).

East-West Center, *Asia-Pacific Report: Trends, Issues, Challenges* (1986).

East-West Center, *The East-West Center and the Pacific* (1980).

Graves, Howard, "Compact Implemented for the Marshalls," Associated Press, (October 23, 1986).

Greenleaf, Charles, Statement Before the House Foreign Affairs Sub-Committee on East Asian and Pacific Affairs, (September 10, 1986).

Holbrooke, Richard, assistant secretary of state for East Asian and Pacific affairs, Statement before the Senate Foreign Relations Sub-Committee on East Asian and Pacific Affairs (July 31, 1978).

Honolulu Star-Bulletin, "Fiji's Prime Minister Praises East-West Center" (June 27, 1985).

Honolulu Star-Bulletin and Advertiser, "Schultz' Trip Signals Pacific Concerns," (June 22, 1986).

Islands Business Magazine, "Forum Changes Tack," (August 1986).

Kist, Robert C., "Economic Security Interests in the South Pacific," National Defense University, Washington, D.C. (February 13, 1986).

Lini, Walter, *Beyond Pandemonium: From the New Hebrides to Vanuatu*, Asia-Pacific Books, (1980).

Lyons, James, "A Peace-time Strategy for the Pacific," Naval War College, Newport, Rhode Island (June 19, 1986).

Pacific Magazine, "U.S. Policy in the Pacific Island Region" (May 4, 1984).

Pacific Island Monthly, "The World's Most Over Coordinated Region," (August 1986).

Rogers, Robert F., *Guam's Search for Commonwealth Status*, University of Guam (1984).

Sigur, Gaston J. Assistant Secretary for East Asian and Pacific Affairs, "The Strategic Importance of the Emerging Pacific," U.S. Department of State, Current Policy no. 871 (September 29, 1986).

Sun, Lena, "No Island Is an Island," *The Washington Post*, National Weekly Edition (July 7, 1986).

Vagi, Legu L., "The Challenge of the Expanding Pacific," Washington, D.C. (October 1, 1986).

Watson, Trevor, "Fishing Agreement Brings Back Lost Goodwill in the Pacific," Associated Press, (August 21, 1986).

Part *II*

*Impact of Market
Conditions and
Institutional
Arrangements on
Commodities and
Primary Products*

Chapter 5

Domestic and International Constraints on Market Development

Rasheed A. Ali

Domestic constraints on development

The island territories of the South Pacific region share a number of common characteristics. With the exception of Papua New Guinea, they are small in size with few natural resources and geographically dispersed over large areas of the ocean. Development is a relatively new phenomenon with a large part of the island economies dominated by the noncash, subsistence sector. With small domestic markets they rely heavily on international trade to meet the needs of their people and to finance much needed development programs.

The world market environment places the island territories in a disadvantageous position both for imports and exports. The reliance on imports for a wide range of goods from foodstuff to heavy machinery places a heavy burden on the countries' financial resources. Being small buyers, they have little ability to influence the price of imported goods. Distance from the major metropolitan markets is reflected in added freight costs and added costs of imported goods. While most of the countries have adopted the goal of achieving self sufficiency in food items, the extent of success in import substitution has been limited.

Development efforts in the island countries focus on the need to develop exports as a way of broadening the foreign exchange base. Here again success to date has been limited. Most of the countries depend on a narrow range of exports, primarily of agricultural products, and their overall contribution has been far below expectation. The ability to successfully export commodities and to increase the range of such exportable commodities has met with numerous problems and constraints. These problems arise both on the domestic as well as the international front.

Among the domestic problems are internal transport problems, supply irregularity, diseconomies of scale, and inadequate marketing organization and quality control measures. The island territories, generally speaking, have to contend with internal transport problems in bringing produce from the outlying islands to the main centers for export. The irregularity and type of shipping services available act as a serious constraint. In addition, the scattered locations, the long distances over which the produce has to be transported, and the small produce volume increase the unit cost of the product.

Commercial production and marketing of most agricultural commodities is a high cost operation. Generally the small holder structure of production for most commodities means the economies of scale associated with large scale production are seldom achievable. Furthermore, with production based on small holder systems, continuity and regularity of supply has been difficult to maintain. Supply is also affected by adverse weather conditions and more particularly by ravaging cyclones that appear to have increased in frequency in recent years, notably in Fiji. A major problem in the development of export commodities has been the lack of proper marketing organizations and mechanisms to ensure that quality parameters are met.

World market constraints

I have touched briefly on the internal constraints that hinder or limit the opportunity for development of export commodities. However, the overriding problem of the South Pacific territories is the exposure to the vagaries of world market conditions and in some cases the difficulty of remaining competitive under distorted market conditions.

South Pacific Territories export commodities on both free markets (for example, coconut oil and cocoa) and distorted markets (for example, sugar). Both markets bring with them special sets of problems. In particular, under both sets of market conditions, the countries are so small that they have no ability to influence the level of world prices. Generally, they start off from a distinct disadvantage of high unit cost of production due to diseconomies associated with lower volume of production and high freight costs owing to their considerable distance from the main market centers. Prolonged depressions of markets, which are common occurrences, cause considerable hardships to the economies dependent on a narrow base of agricultural commodities. The effects are so severe that in some cases (for example, copra) the industries cannot regain their former position of significance.

It could be said that where the market operates freely, the countries trading within its framework should be prepared to accept the realities of the market situation and make such adjustments as are necessary. However, such adjustments are not easy to make when there are few, if any, cash crop alternatives.

The world sugar market and the Fiji sugar industry

What can be said of cases in which free interaction of the forces of supply and demand are tampered with? Sugar is a good case in point where the market for developing countries is virtually devastated because of interference with free market mechanisms by major industrial powers. To illustrate this point, I intend to discuss the case of sugar as a product of Fiji and the problems encountered with this commodity in international trading.

Sugar has been the main crop and dominant foreign-exchange earner for Fiji for over one hundred years. Since 1973 sugar milling operations have been in local hands, previously being controlled by the CSR Company of Australia. The development and fortunes of the Fiji economy have been linked to the developments in the sugar industry. The Fiji Sugar Corporation, Ltd. (FSC), which is majority owned by the government, is the sole miller in Fiji, operating four sugar mills and the rail transportation infrastructure. The mills have a combined capacity to handle annually in excess of 525,000 tons of sugar. The highest level of sugar production was achieved last year when the sugar industry produced 502,000 tons of sugar from about 4 million tons of cane.

Unlike the milling business, which is controlled by a single miller (FSC), cane used for the manufacture of raw sugar is grown by some 22,000 individual growers, with an average-sized holding of about 4.5 hectares. The cane crushing season lasts about seven months (normally from May to December) on a 24-hour, seven-days-a-week basis. The small holder system of cane farming calls for a considerable degree of organization and coordination to ensure that the business of sugar manufacturing is successfully undertaken.

The marketing of Fiji's sugar is undertaken by a separate organization, the Fiji Sugar Marketing Co., Ltd. (FSM), which is wholly government owned. FSM discharges its role as the agent of the Fiji Sugar Corporation.

Sugar enjoys a distinct position of advantage in Fiji. It is climatically, agronomically, and culturally suited to Fiji and despite ravaging cyclones and droughts in some years, the sugar industry in Fiji has shown considerable resilience and has maintained production levels to meet export commitments. Fiji sugar is reputed for its high quality, and an elaborate infrastructure exists for marketing sugar. Fiji is one of the lowest-cost producers of cane and sugar in the world. The small-holder system of farming is a major source of strength to the sugar industry, making cane farming more resilient and cost effective. More particularly, because of the opportunity for utilization of family labor, adjustments in the cost of production are possible in times of depressed market conditions.

Fiji also enjoys a distinct position of advantage because of the existence of secure and favorably priced markets for a large part of its production.

Fiji exports about 95 percent of its annual production of about 480,000 tons to overseas markets. About 65 percent of exports currently go under long term arrangements or at special prices and 35 percent at the world market price. Fiji, like other African, Caribbean and Pacific sugar countries (ACP), has a long-term arrangement with the European Economic Community (EEC) countries under the Lome Convention. This arrangement, which is for an indefinite duration, provides Fiji guaranteed access to the EEC for 174,000 tons of sugar annually. The price paid for these exports is linked to the price paid to the EEC's highly subsidized beet sugar producers. Thus it has been significantly more than the prices prevailing on the world market in recent years and above the costs of production. Fiji also derives satisfactory returns from sugar sales to Malaysia, New Zealand, and the United States, particularly in comparison to the dismal returns from world market sales. Long-term agreements and special arrangements form the revenue backbone of the sugar industry in Fiji. They have helped to give Fiji a considerable measure of income stability, particularly in times of low world market prices.

The major problem for Fiji arises from its exposure to the world market for about 35 percent of its annual production and the disappointingly low returns from the market. The world sugar market has generally followed a cyclical pattern with long periods of troughs followed by short periods of peaks. The last price peak was in 1980-81. Following this, prices began a declining trend reaching an all-time low in 1985. While there has been some improvement since then, sugar prices have not picked up to any real extent. The current price of around seven cents per pound is too low and not sufficient to meet the cost of production of even the most efficient producers. The world sugar market is saddled with a high level of stocks, and unless they are reduced to reasonable levels, the market will continue to be depressed.

Let me now turn briefly to some of the characteristics of the world sugar market. Most of the sugar produced in the world is consumed in producer countries. This means that a small proportion of world production is traded on the world market. Even of the quantity that crosses borders, a fair proportion is covered under special arrangements, as in the case of ACP with EEC countries and Cuba with Russia. In the year 1985-86, raw sugar exports to the world market were about 18 million tons, which represented about 18 percent of world production. The world market is thus a residual market prone to major fluctuations in prices even with minor changes in supply and demand. While the market potentially provides for both high and low prices, the situation effectively has been prolonged periods of low prices. This is so because surplus stocks continue at high levels, and no major initiatives have been taken to reduce production and allow stocks to reach acceptable levels.

The world market demand for sugar is inelastic in that changes in prices do not affect the overall demand for sugar to any significant extent. In fact, in the more developed countries, per capita consumption has declined. The situation of production increases in the face of static or declining demand has led to a buildup of sugar stocks and to the poor state of the market.

On the international front, two critical factors have had enormous bearing in changing the nature of the world sugar market. The first is the emergence of the European Economic Community from a net importer of sugar in the 1960s to the world's second largest exporter of sugar (after Cuba) and the largest exporter of sugar to the world market.

The other factor is the advent of high fructose corn syrups and other artificial sweeteners, notably in the United States, which have taken over a sigificant proportion of the world sweetener market, effectively reducing the traditional sugar demand. Furthermore, the policies adopted by the United States have led to an increase in its domestic sugar production.

Institutional arrangements

It is of concern that these developments have occurred and persist even though the world sugar market has been depressed for several years. Indeed, these factors are primarily responsible for the poor state of the world sugar market.

The EEC countries have instituted arrangements to maintain sugar prices in the community at well above free market levels. At these attractive prices, the EEC's beet sugar producers have the incentive to maintain production levels at well above consumption requirements. While it is known that this is distorting the market and obstructing the free interplay of the forces of supply and demand, no constructive action has been taken to address the situation.

The United States is also heavily subsidizing its producers by maintaining domestic prices at unrealistically high levels. The highly attractive prices have acted as an incentive to increase domestic sugar production and have led to the emergence of artificial sweeteners and a decrease in overall consumption. The situation is such that the United States' import market for sugar has been a shrinking one. United States' imports have declined from 5 million tons in 1981 (that is, the year prior to the imposition of import quotas) to 1 million tons in 1987, with indications that if the current trend continues, imports would be eliminated.

I have gone to some length in describing the change in the market situation because therein lies the explanation for the excessive availability of sugar relative to demand and consequently the poor state of the market. Under current conditions and with the unresponsiveness of the EEC and the United States to the plight of other sugar producers, the prospects for any significant improvement in sugar prices appear bleak. The burden of adjustment falls on the world's cane sugar exporters, the group who can least afford it. It will be noted that attempts to control world sugar prices through the mechanism of the International Sugar Agreement had also failed owing to lack of cooperation from the major world sugar producers and in particular, the EEC. On the one hand, the EEC offers Fiji and other ACP countries their best market measured in terms of both quantity and price. On the other hand, because they dump their surpluses on the free market below cost, they are also Fiji's and other cane producers' biggest enemy.

What are the solutions?

Undoubtedly, the South Pacific territories face a number of problems in their efforts to develop and diversify their export base. There are some critical constraints on the domestic front that no doubt have to be overcome if success is to be achieved in penetrating overseas markets. However, despite measures to resolve the domestic constraints, the countries have to contend with the reality of world market conditions and the various institutional arrangements that affect the free operation of the market.

In the case of sugar discussed earlier, the market for which is severely distorted, there is little the countries themselves can do apart from ensuring that they are reliable, efficient, and low-cost producers of the commodity. The unfortunate reality is that, if the world sugar prices continue to be depressed much longer, the industry's viability will fall in jeopardy leading to curtailment of the operation and ultimately to complete closure. Some of the sugar industries in the world have already suffered this fate. There is a lot that major industrial powers like the EEC and the United States can do to lift the sugar market out of the doldrums. This would no doubt mean taking decisions likely to be unpalatable to their domestic producers. We can only look forward expectantly to the future for some policy changes that would help the sugar market.

As for the products that are freely traded on the world market, the key for the South Pacific territories is to make their products internationally price competitive, that is to say, they must be efficiently produced. Where this is not possible, consideration has to be given to diversifying into products that are more competitive. The countries of the South Pacific are conscious of the need to diversify but have inevitably run into problems where it is a question of international competition.

With the difficulties involved in maintaining international competitiveness, the South Pacific Territories must of necessity seek and rely on special, preferential arrangements with the developed countries. A significant preferential trading arrangement is the South Pacific Regional Trade and Economic Cooperation Agreement (SPARTECA). SPARTECA provides duty-free access in respect of virtually all primary industry commodities to Australia and New Zealand. With the existence of SPARTECA, Fiji and other Pacific countries could competitively sell fresh tropical products in the large urban markets of Australia and New Zealand. No doubt the opportunities provided to SPARTECA will be exploited by the South Pacific territories. In addition, the countries will need to seek more preferential arrangements of the type that they can take full advantage of.

The development dilemma facing the South Pacific countries has led to suggestions by some experts that the best opportunities for export development lie in the production and export of high-value, specialized products, for example, tropical fruits and horticultural products. It is suggested that in this way advantages of climate, off-season location, and trade agreements can be maximized and the disadvantages of diseconomies of scale and distance from major markets can be minimized. Success with this approach would depend on the quality and reliability of supply and the establishment of an organized marketing system and supporting infrastructure. No doubt, this strategy will also be actively pursued.

Conclusion

Throughout the world, countries dependent on agricultural products and other commodities are forced to live with the constraints of adverse and uncertain market conditions as well as market distortions brought about by institutional arrangements and the trade policies of developed countries. The problems, of course, are more severe for small countries struggling to develop their countries against a multitude of domestic and international constraints. The complexity of the problems and the difficulty of finding solutions are fully recognized. As the search for solutions continues, forums such as the Global Community Forum have a useful role to play in generating ideas and strategies beneficial to the countries caught in the development dilemma.

Chapter 6

The Commodity Problem with Special Reference to the South Pacific

Yasukichi Yasuba

It was only fifteen years ago that the Club of Rome warned about the possibility of resource shortage and predicted the probability of catastrophe in the near future.[1] The oil crises appeared to fulfill their prophecy. Through most of the 1970s, commodity prices were high, and proposals were made to stabilize their prices at high levels.

But then, from the end of the 1970s, the prices of virtually all nonoil commodities started to decline By 1986 average real prices (deflated by the price of the manufactures) of nonoil commodities went down to 60 percent of the average 1956-86 (See Figure 6.1). Beverages whose prices were relatively strong due to the bad coffee crop in Brazil were the only exception. Food was particularly hard hit.

Figure 6.1
Real non-oil commodity prices
1957-1987

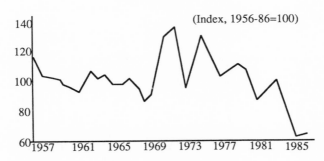

(Index, 1956-86=100)

I.M.F., *World Economic Outlook*, April 1987, p. 94.

Population continued to increase as the Club of Rome had predicted and the demand for food increased accordingly. The supply, however, increased dramatically in response to pessimism and also owing to the price support policy of industrial and semi-industrial countries.

The so-called Green Revolution for rice and wheat increased the yield of these commodities in many developing countries. The increase was particularly noteworthy in Asia, but even in Africa, where some countries suffer from famine, production increased substantially. (See Table 6.1) The problem in Africa is not so much that of absolute shortage but that of the shortage of effective demand caused by maldistribution of income.

Table 6.1
Yield and production of rice and wheat
1979-81 and 1986

	Yield (kg/ha)		Production (1,000 MT)	
	1979-81	1986	1979-81	1986
Rice				
World	2,757	3,291	396,315	476,395
Africa	1,755	1,828	8,608	9,991
N. America	4,395	4,761	9,148	8,262
S. America	1,837	2,231	13,335	15,534
Asia	2,805	3,377	360,078	437,201
Europe	5,132	5,538	1,879	2,191
Wheat				
World	1,885	2,306	443,509	527,377
Africa	1,096	1,366	8,953	11,437
N. America	2,174	2,332	89,470	92,743
S. America	1,316	1,709	12,235	17,210
Asia	1,700	2,242	136,328	186,976
Europe	3,601	4,470	91,887	116,235
Oceania	1,281	1,553	14,777	17,784
U.S.S.R.	1,511	1,742	89,858	85,000

Source: Food and Agriculture Organization of the United Nations, *Monthly Bulletin of Statistics,* (December 1986), 14 and 17.

It may be noted that, as a result of land improvement, acreage has also increased in many regions of the world, especially in Africa, Asia, and Europe. As a result, despite the cutback in North America, the total acreage in the world for these major crops has increased. North America has a vast withdrawn from cultivation, and South America appears to have a large tract of land that can be used in the future, thanks to technical progress.

In the case of agricultural raw materials, forest products, and minerals and metals, world demand has shrunk in relative terms. According to an IMF study the amount of raw material needed for a given unit of economic output has decreased by 60 percent since 1900. Japanese experience has particularly been noteworthy. Between 1973 and 1984, the amount of raw material used for a given unit of industrial production decreased by 40 percent.[2] The once-thriving Japanese production of industrial raw materials, such as steel and aluminum, is in a deep recession. High-tech industries and services use very little raw materials. Slumping capital formation also has reduced the demand for iron and steel.

Except for Japan and the U.S.S.R., the import market for food has almost disappeared. Western Europe as a whole has already become a net exporter of food, competing with the United States. The People's Republic of China and India are likely to become food exporters in the near future. Most of the resource-rich countries of Southeast Asia have become almost self-sufficient, if not exporters. It is true that a number of developing countries still import food, but it is becoming more and more difficult for them to earn sufficient foreign exchange.

The slump in commodity prices spread recently to crude oil. The price of oil was kept artificially high in the 1970s and the early 1980s as a result of the cutback of exports by the OPEC countries. This was made possible to some extent by the cartel agreement but mainly by the drastic reduction of exports by Saudi Arabia. By 1985, however, Saudi Arabia could no longer accept the reduction of revenue and discarded the role of a "swing producer."

This change of Saudi policy immediately reduced the spot oil price that became lower than $10 a barrel in August 1986. Then OPEC members tried to meet several times to restore the cartel agreement. After the interim agreement in August, they adopted two decisions of far-reaching importance. First, new production quotas were agreed upon for the first half of 1987, reducing the total output by nearly 10 percent. Second, official average export prices of $18 a barrel were introduced.

The fall of oil prices is estimated to have increased demand by about 2.5 percent in 1986 in industrialized countries. Oil consumption also rose in some oil-importing developing countries, but some of them have recently taken steps to curtail the rise in demand.[3]

On the supply side, the OPEC share recovered somewhat in 1986. The total exports from OPEC countries is estimated to have risen by about 15 percent. Total non-OPEC output declined somewhat in more than a decade. The decline represented to some extent the shutting down of small wells, mostly in the United States.[4]

In the case of crude oil, it was possible to recover the price to about $18 per barrel. Even though it came down somewhat recently, the oil price is expected to rise further in the middle of the 1990s owing to the absolute shortage of the reserve.[5] Oil is the exception, however. In the case of other commodities, the producers have no effective means of restricting the supply. In many cases, a large number of small producers may even have to try to increase output because the prices are low, initiating an immiserizing growth.

Since the optimism in the 1970s was strong, many countries and producers tried to increase output with a thrust. The resulting technological breakthroughs and a large-scale investment prepared a way for a sustained increase in the supply of agricultural commodities. Ongoing progress in biotechnology may introduce a further increase in productivity. Technological progress in other fields may also slow down the increase in demand for industrial materials.

Thus, Barbara Insel declared that "we have entered an era of permanent grain surpluses."[6] Peter F. Drucker has gone further and said that the "primary products economy has come 'uncoupled' from the industrial economy."[7] Even though the forces of supply and demand may eventually eliminate the excess supply and bring back the equilibrium, it may take a long time for such a market-oriented solution to take place.

Small-scale subsistence suppliers in developing countries, even though they will have to suffer in the meantime, may be able to survive or convert to producers of manufactures and services.

What is more bothersome is the fate of commercial producers who have expanded production in the last 15 years based on borrowed funds, expecting the good prices of the 1970s to continue. Their bankruptcies may start a chain reaction of bankruptcies in the banking sector triggering a worldwide depression like that of the 1930s. The problem is so urgent that it may be wise to adopt some impromptu measures to avoid disaster. For example, an international fund may be established for buying up food in the market to be given to starving developing countries in sub-Sahara Africa. The food may be given in the form of the school lunch program to middle-income developing countries whose children are going hungry because of the maldistribution of income. The program may also ease the balance of payment problem of a number of countries.

South Pacific islands depend heavily on the export of primary products as shown in Table 6.2. The Background Document of this forum states that prices of the exports products "have been extremely low over the past five years or so."[8]

This is certainly true with sugar, which is Fiji's major export. For other exports, the picture is not so clear. Compared with those of 1980, the 1985 prices are currently lower, but compared with 1975, the current prices are generally higher. In any case, the 1985 prices of exports of the South Pacific islands are better than those of major trade items such as wheat, rice, and maize (See Table 6.3). Even though we have to be careful about the interpretation of price indexes because they depend crucially on the choice of the base year, we should at least be able to say that the South Pacific island economy is yet to be "uncoupled" from the industrial economy.

Table 6.2
Exports of major South Pacific islands
by principal products, 1981
(U.S. $1,000)

	American Samoa	Fiji	New Caledonia	Papua N.G.	Solomon Islands	Vanuatu	Western Samoa
Fish and Seafoods	166,170	17,515	33	34,838	22,182	---	---
Sugar	---	137,043	---	---	---	---	---
Coffee, tea, etc.	---	2,696	371	150,400	902	1,108	1,238
Copra	---	---	13	26,187	8,131	9,473	3,382
Wood and By-products	---	2,063	---	57,380	16,232	189	249
Minerals	---	12,376	222,371	388,898	525	---	---
Total	173,110	280,175	286,938	733,646	58,136	25,067	9,612

Source: "The Pacific Islands in the Context of the Pacific Basin," Background Document for the Global community forum, 1987, 85-86.

Table 6.3
Index of commodity prices
1975-1985
(1975 = 100)

	1980	1981	1982	1983	1984	1985
World Commodities						
Wheat	115.8	117.2	107.4	105.4	102.2	91.1
Rice	119.4	132.9	90.8	76.2	69.5	59.9
Maize	103.4	109.0	86.9	111.4	112.4	91.7
South Pacific Products						
Bananas	152.6	163.2	152.4	174.5	150.3	154.7
Coffee	207.9	159.8	173.3	176.5	194.9	184.1
Copra	177.0	148.0	122.7	193.9	277.4	150.9
Logs	285.8	214.0	211.9	202.1	221.6	196.0
Nickel	142.6	130.2	105.8	102.2	104.0	107.2
Palm Oil	111.9	103.7	88.1	92.4	137.4	104.5
Sugar	105.6	96.0	50.1	51.7	39.2	29.3

Source: International Monetary Fund, *International Financial Statistics 1986 Yearbook* (Washington, D.C.).

Notes

1. Dennis L. Meadows et al., *The Limit to Growth: A Report for the Club of Rome's Project on the Predicament of Mankind* (New York: Universal Books, 1972).
2. Peter F. Drucker, "The Changed World Economy," *Foreign Affairs,* (Spring 1986), p. 773.
3. International Monetary Fund; *World Economic Outlook*, (April 1987), 99.
4. *World Economic Outlook;* 99.
5. Akihiro Amano, "Sekai Sekiyu Jukyu Model Niyoru Sekiyu Kakaku Yosoku" [Production of Oil Price Based on a World Demand-Supply Model of Oil], a paper presented at a Conference on Energy System and Economy, Tokyo, 1987.
6. Barbara Insel, "A World Awash in Grain," *Foreign Affairs*, (Spring 1985), 892.
7. Drucker, "The Changed World Economy;" 768.
8. "The Pacific Islands in the Context of the Pacific Basin," Background Document for the Global Community Forum, 1987, 83.

Chapter 7

South Pacific Trade and Development Assistance

Peter Drysdale

The theme of this conference is Pacific cooperation and development. There are two important aspects of this subject that deserve attention, as we meet here in the South Pacific. The first relates to South Pacific trade and external economic interests and the relationship between those interests and the economic cooperation and development prospects of South Pacific countries. The second relates to the broader issue of Pacific economic cooperation among the larger economies across the Pacific--the United States, Japan, East Asia, and the Western Pacific countries, including the Association of Southeast Asian Nations, Australia and New Zealand, and the South Pacific island countries. These two aspects have thus far been treated somewhat separately. In this paper, I shall suggest that there are significant links between these two aspects of Pacific economic cooperation and development, and I shall try to identify some of those links briefly.

Without exception, South Pacific countries rely upon trade in primary commodities for a large proportion of their gross domestic product. External earnings from primary commodity trade are supplemented (to varying degrees) by remittances, tourism, and external assistance. Exports comprise around 40-50 percent of the value of the gross domestic product for most countries in the region.

Western Pacific primary commodity exporters (South Pacific countries included) have suffered a huge decline in their export prices and terms of trade over the last few years. Table 7.1 sets out the commodity concentration in South Pacific trade and the relative importance of particular commodity exports to particular South Pacific countries. Volatility in the prices of primary commodities is an endemic economic and social management problem for small primary export-dependent countries, but the severity of this problem in the last decade or so merits special attention, not only because of the significant economic adjustments that have had to be managed but also because of the social and political adjustments they in turn have set in motion

Table 7.1
Exports of primary products from Pacific island countries
(1981-83 average: U.S. million)

	Papua New Guinea	Fiji	Solomon Islands	Vanuatu	Other Oceanic	Total
Copper	288.8	*	*	*	*	288.8
Gold	230.7	14.1	*	*	*	244.8
Sugar	0.9	132.8	*	*	*	133.8
Coffee	109.8	*	*	0.1	*	109.9
Phosphate	*	*	*	*	106.7	106.7
Timer	71.1	2.0	21.4	0.8	0.9	96.2
Cocoa	47.8	0.3	1.3	1.3	1.6	52.3
Copra	25.0	*	8.4	10.9	5.6	49.9
Palm Oil	26.3	*	7.5	*	*	33.8
Copra Oil	19.7	8.2	*	0.1	5.0	32.9
Tea	10.7	0.1	*	*	*	10.8
Rubber	3.2	*	*	*	*	3.2
Beef	*	*	*	1.2	*	1.2
Bananas	*	*	*	*	1.0	1.0
Rice	*	*	0.7	*	*	0.7
Tobacco	0.2	*	*	*	*	0.2
Subtotal	834.2	157.5	39.3	14.4	120.8	1,166.2
Other	186.9	153.5	22.4	14.0	27.4	386.1
Total	1,021.1	293.0	61.7	28.4	148.2	1,552.3

*Zero or less than half the unit shown.
  Exports of gold derived from national sources.

Source: World Bank, *Commodity Trade and Price Trends,* (Washington, D.C.: Johns Hopkins University Press, 1986).

Population continued to increase as the Club of Rome had predicted and the demand for food increased accordingly. The supply, however, increased dramatically in response to pessimism and also owing to the price support policy of industrial and semi-industrial countries.

The so-called Green Revolution for rice and wheat increased the yield of these commodities in many developing countries. The increase was particularly noteworthy in Asia, but even in Africa, where some countries suffer from famine, production increased substantially, (see Table 7.1). The problem in Africa is not so much one of absolute shortage but one of the shortage of effective demand caused by maldistribution of income.

This problem has not only affected the small South Pacific primary commodity exporters but it has also affected all primary commodity exporters in the Western Pacific. It has exposed the political fragilities in the Philippines. Low copper and other export prices have put the economy and social system of Papua New Guinea through an extreme test--a test that, it should be added happily, that country came through with merit but not without difficulty. It has required big adjustments in Indonesia, and even in my own secure and rich country, the social, political, and economic adjustment has been great

Depressed international commodity markets have affected South Pacific countries directly, through reduced foreign earnings, and indirectly, through the reduced capacity for development assistance of the primary donors to the region (Australia and New Zealand), themselves struggling with the budgetary adjustment to lower international earnings. This was an extremely serious problem from 1980 to 1985, although Australia has redirected aid programs toward the South Pacific in the last year or so. Table 7.2 sets out the scale and structure of aid disbursements to South Pacific nations in 1980 and 1985 and reveals the importance of Australia and New Zealand to the region and the concentration in aid flows from other metropolitan countries.

In broad terms, the collapse in commodity prices has wiped between 5 and 15 percent off regional incomes in the last few years. Even if the qualification that price performance has been somewhat different across commodities is accepted, it does not alter this broad picture. This is an extreme adjustment to have had to make. It is much more serious a problem, for example, than the rich industrial countries faced in consequence of the oil price hikes in the 1970s, when the terms of trade shift against them only reduced income by around 2-3 percent.

The issues

There are three levels at which this problem must be managed in terms of economic policy. First, there is the issue of what responsibilities, if any, the large developed-country consumers of the main primary commodity exports can exercise to control or suppress the price and earnings instability from which suppliers suffer. This point is made forcefully in the paper prepared by Richard A. Ali dealing with the case of sugar trade. The impact of European, U.S. and Japanese support programs on world market prices is much more damaging than the benefit derived from partial access for some countries to the protected European or U.S. market. The overwhelming evidence suggests that the main action the large consumer countries can take to improve the international commodity market situation is to modify their own primary

Table 7.2
Net disbursement of official development assistance:
US $ million

	Total	Total	Australia	New Zealand	United Kingdom	EC	Japan	France	United States	Other
	1980	1985	1985	1985	1985	1985	1985	1985	1985	1985
Cook Islands	10.7	9.7	0.79	6.99	—	—	0.34	—	—	1.58
Fiji	36.1	31.9	10.03	3.39	1.81	3.60	8.15	—	1.00	3.92
Kiribati	19.2	12.0	2.56	0.87	4.57	0.48	2.80	—	—	0.72
Nauru		0.1	0.01	—	—	—	—	—	—	0.05
Niue	3.7	3.5	0.06	3.45	—	—	0.01	—	—	0.02
Pacific Is. (Trust Tr)	109.3	159.3	0.18	—	—	—	3.74	—	154.0	1.38
Papua New Guinea	325.9	258.9	226.85	2.86	0.09	4.15	3.95	1.14	1.00	18.86
Polynesia, French	159.5	172.0	0.12	—	—	1.23	0.12	170.21	—	0.32
Solomon Islands	44.5	20.8	5.60	0.59	5.28	1.52	0.81	—	1.00	6.00
Tokelau	1.9	1.8	—	1.58	—	—	—	—	—	0.22
Tonga	16.4	13.6	4.85	2.65	0.17	0.77	1.33	0.35	—	3.48
Tuvalu	4.9	3.3	0.91	0.41	1.73	0.03	0.07	—	—	0.15
Vanuatu	44.0	21.8	4.39	1.04	6.55	1.11	0.75	5.88	—	2.08
Wallis and Futuna	8.3	0.2	—	—	—	0.20	—	-0.02	—	—
Western Samoa	25.7	19.4	5.34	3.77	0.06	1.69	1.82	0.05	1.00	5.67
Oceania unallocated	16.4	26.2	6.83	8.49	0.83	—	0.20	2.40	7.00	0.45
Total	1024.4	899.9	268.60	36.09	21.09	14.97	24.09	325.11	165.00	44.95

Source: OECD, Geographic Dstribution of Fnancial Fows to Dveloping Countries, 1982-85, Paris OECD, 1987, 21 for aggregate figures in 1980 and 1985. Figures for bilateral donors are sourced from the OECD's Development Assistance Committee.

commodity control and stabilization schemes so as to prevent the export of price instability. Europe, Japan, and the United States all operate primary commodity market control arrangements, the principal effect of which is to increase international market instability.[1]

It might appear at first sight that such arrangements have little impact on the export instability endured by South Pacific exporters, whose main agricultural exports are sugar and vegetable oils. However, the substitution effects from commodities produced under industrial country protection schemes are great, and South Pacific exporters suffer policy-induced export instability in the same way as do other efficient primary commodity exporters. They are similar problems to those endured by efficient exporters of grain and temperate zone agricultural commodities, the distorted markets for which Yasukichi Yasuba's paper describes. These policies are economically inefficient and politically negligent of the interest of countries vulnerable because of the absolute need to specialize in trade.

Second, there is the issue of efficient management of instability problems in the small exporter economies. There are two aspects of this problem: getting macroeconomic management (monetary and fiscal policies) right; and managing domestic commodity marketing and stabilization arrangements so as not to compromise economic efficiency over the commodity cycle. Commodity production cannot and should not be permanently subsidized. Commodity quality differences need proper rewards and incentive. Again Ali's paper makes these points forcefully. Among all the South Pacific countries, Papua New Guinea probably manages this aspect best, in the structure of the marketing and commodity stabilization arrangements it has established. This fact has stood its economy in good stead over tough times in recent years. Elsewhere the record is variable and marketing arrangements in some countries involve considerable inefficiencies. On these questions of policy and institutional reform, there is much scope for exchange of ideas and experience within the South Pacific region.

The third issue relates to the opportunity for expanding market access through extending free trade arrangements. The South Pacific Regional Trade and Economic Cooperation Agreement (SPARTECA) was a limited first step, but the extension of free trade into Australia and New Zealand is a policy priority that, I hope, at least Australia is coming to recognize. A more important dimension, however, is the effective representation of South Pacific trading interests in broader regional and global forums. Here there is opportunity for developing a common approach and the more effective representation of common trade and economic interests by the South Pacific and other Western Pacific primary commodity exporters.

Trade policy initiatives are obviously only one part of the overall approach necessary for effective economic cooperation and development in the South Pacific. Trade cooperation needs to be combined with development assistance for social and economic infrastructure, research into agricultural and other problems affecting the long-term economic viability of the South Pacific economy, and other important elements, such as education assistance, the freer movement of labor and remittance income within the region. These latter problems are not easy policy problems, the burden of which will continue to fall on Australia and New Zealand. A policy approach towards the big South Pacific countries (Papua New Guinea and Fiji) has to be developed within an overall framework that accommodates the particular problems of the smaller, less economically viable countries.

As more aid becomes available from other donors, such as Japan and the multilateral institutions, the need for a new consultative and coordination mechanism will become more urgent. The region has scarce administrative resources. Coordination of aid programs through a South Pacific aid consultative mechanism will protect South Pacific island nations from administrative and economic waste, as well as serve to strengthen further institutions within the region itself, such as the South Pacific Economic Commission (SPEC).

Financial assistance alone will not correct the problems identified here. Indeed, additional funding may simply lead to economic waste, domestic economic loss, and the corruption of economic management systems. A much more important requirement from developed countries is policy change aimed at improving the operation of free international markets (not treating international markets as "residuals" through which domestic adjustments can be avoided). In South Pacific primary commodity exporting countries, support for marketing arrangements that give proper weight to economic viability and incentives remains a key requirement, alongside support for extending the regional market and the representation of the region's economic interests through regional and international institutions.

The South Pacific and Pacific economic cooperation

The issues on which I have touched will have to be addressed in relations between South Pacific countries and their major economic partners; that is the proximate area for policy action. But this review of the important issues in the management of the external economic relations of South Pacific nations also suggests a number of connections with the broader interest in Pacific economic cooperation.

The first link relates to the representation of trade policy interests, which South Pacific countries have to some extent in common with other Western Pacific countries. None of the South Pacific countries are members of the General Agreement on Tariffs and Trade (GATT). Fiji has joined with the Cairns Group of efficient agricultural exporters. The South Pacific countries, as a group, may well be able to develop some modest leverage on trade policy matters through association with the discussion of a Pacific trade policy agenda that has been encouraged through the activities of the Pacific Economic Cooperation Conference (PECC) trade policy forum.

There are particular areas of South Pacific interest in development assistance. PECC and its various task force activities provide an opportunity for the informal representation of those interests and open discussion of problems in a way that can serve to build a coalition of support for South Pacific interests in bigger countries, where there are other interests less sensitive to the requirements and circumstances of smaller countries. Fisheries development has been an area of contention in the past; broader Pacific discussion provides an opportunity to counterbalance narrow interests in some large countries and encourage the kind of assistance and arrangements that South Pacific countries want in order to develop their own fisheries resources. The exchange of relevant information and experience in particular areas of policy interest (such as minerals development and trade) or about developments in the international macroeconomy is another benefit from involvement in the PECC activities.

Effective involvement in these broader discussions and consultations on Pacific economic cooperation also require the coordination of regional participation (as it did at the beginning in the first Canberra meeting), preferably through SPEC, taking account of particular country interests in particular issues in the country composition of participation.

The PECC process does not have its effect directly on policy. It is a nongovernmental body, involving participation by senior officials, industry people, and researchers, all in their private capacities. It does, however, provide the opportunity for building up coalitions of common policy interest and the capacity to anticipate and avoid problems among the countries involved. This is proving to be its great strength, for example in the way in which it has encouraged some of the trade policy problems of Pacific countries, referred to above, to be addressed in negotiations through the new GATT round.

Perspective

Other papers presented to this conference have stressed the huge problems that have to be managed among the big economic powers in the Pacific--the United States, Japan, and the newly industrializing nations of East Asia--and in relations with Europe. The macroeconomic and international payments imbalances and economic recession have combined to weaken commodity markets, aggravate protectionism in industrial countries, and expose the distortions in world agricultural trade.

The small countries of the South Pacific inevitably feel a sense of powerlessness in the face of problems on this scale and beyond influence. In my own country, there is some of the same feeling. But what these problems and their scale suggest is the importance of working together so that we can seek solutions that will protect the interests of smaller and weaker countries and the region's economies collectively.

The tensions that are evident in economic relations between the big economies in the Pacific recommend the development and affirmation of agreed-upon policy principles supportive of continuing Pacific trade growth and development, not bilateral deals and settlements between the big economic partners that damage third (and smaller) country interests through the export of domestic adjustment problems.

The framework that is being established through the Pacific Economic Cooperation Conference seems to be making a modest but effective contribution toward meeting some of these challenges. South Pacific nations as a group are likely, in this context, to find growing value in the PECC process.

Note

1. Kym Anderson and Rod Tyers, "European Community Grain and Meat Policies: Effects on International Prices, Trade and Welfare," *European Review of Agricultural Economics* 2:4 (1984): 366-94; Kym Anderson and Yujiro Hayami, *The Political Economy and Agricultural Protection.* (Sydney, Allen and Unwin; 1986), especially chap. 5; Kym Anderson and Rod Tyers, "Agricultural Policies of Industrial Countries and Their Effects on Traditional Food Exporters," *Economic Record* 62: 179 (December 1986) 385-99; and World Bank, *World Development Report 1986,* (New York, Oxford University Press 1986) table 6.9, 131.

Part *III*

Technology as a Transformational Resource

Chapter 8

Appropriate Technology and Economic Growth

C. J. Maiden

By technology we mean a body of existing knowledge that is relevant to a particular field of practical endeavor. The knowledge may derive mainly from science but may also involve aspects of traditional arts and crafts. In discussing technology as a transformational resource we are considering the economic, environmental, social, and cultural impact of technology on a society.

From the viewpoint of economic performance, there is good evidence that it is those nations that have invested heavily in science and technology that are leading the way. In particular, OECD data show that there is a strong correlation between gross domestic product (GDP) per capita and the development and application of technology in a society. Of course, the Pacific Ocean washes ashore on countries in all stages of development, including five of the OECD nations, and some technologies will be more appropriate than others to enhance the economic performance of a particular country.

How can appropriate technology be identified, developed, and innovatively applied in Pacific island countries?

For developing countries with small populations, the term "appropriate technology" has come to have a widely recognized meaning. In general, it involves self-reliance and local production for local needs. The tools and techniques of such appropriate technology (which may be low, medium, or high technology) share characteristics. They

- are low-cost and small-scale,
- use local materials wherever possible,
- employ local skills and labor and create jobs,
- can be understood, controlled, and maintained by communities wherever possible,
- often involve decentralized renewable resources,

- lend themselves to community and cooperative activity,
- do not disrupt the existing social and cultural situation.

To date, the major applications of appropriate technology in the Third World have aimed at meeting the basic human needs of food, shelter, and health. In this respect, there exists a substantial body of instructional literature of the "how-to" kind.

I am not saying that small developing countries should only consider small-scale technologies. There may be justified applications of medium- or large-scale technologies, for example, power stations or export oriented industries. But I believe these should be the exception rather than the rule.

Appropriate technologies for developing countries have been promoted and implemented by official international agencies such as the Asian Development and World banks, UNDP, UNICEF, and the OECD. Regional organizations such as the South Pacific Commission and the South Pacific Bureau of Economic Cooperation have helped, as have government departments and agencies, universities, and church and mission groups from the developed world. In addition, multinational companies and various nongovernment aid organizations have played a role.

However, the more a country can itself identify, develop and apply appropriate technology, the more likely it is to generate and sustain economic growth. For this to happen, innovation and enterprise must be encouraged, modest capital needs to be available, and the society concerned must contain the requisite skills.

Innovation and enterprise seem to flourish best in open societies with good standards of education and economies that contain a healthy private sector sensitive to market forces. The larger the population of a country the easier it should be to create such conditions. In this respect, many of the Pacific island states are at a distinct disadvantage. However, I am sure that it is possible to encourage innovation and entrepreneurial activity in small

Of course, the kind of technology that is appropriate to a particular country is very dependent upon the educational attainment of the population. The higher the attainment, the more sophisticated the technology that can be introduced and handled by that society. By upgrading education, with an emphasis on technical and vocational subjects at the secondary and tertiary levels a country can move up the development scale.

Within the Pacific, particularly among the island states, the development of educational facilities on a regional basis makes a lot of sense. Here the University of the South Pacific is a good example. I would encourage additional initiatives with respect to technical education. Undoubtedly, improved communication systems, based on satellites, will encourage the future development of such regional educational networks.

In further considering educational cooperation, several other activities should be mentioned. The attendance of students from developing countries at educational institutions in the more developed countries that offer courses of specific interest is commonplace and should be encouraged. A good example of such a course is the one-year Diploma of Geothermal Technology offered at my own university, the University of Auckland. This unique course is sponsored by UNDP, the New Zealand Ministry of Foreign Affairs (under the Foreign Aid Vote) and the university. This year, 28 students from 14 countries with an interest in geothermal energy are attending the course. Countries represented in this year's course are Argentina, Costa Rica, Ecuador, El Salvador, Ethiopia, India, Indonesia, Kenya, Mexico, Panama, the Peoples Republic of China, the Philippines, Thailand, and Turkey.

In addition, there is considerable scope for staff and student exchanges between technical institutes, colleges, and universities in and around the Pacific. Also, the secondment of staff from educational institutions in the more developed countries of the region to teach and research in scientific and technical areas of need in less-developed countries can be very helpful. Such assistance is best only on a temporary basis while the local institution builds up its own capability.

Let me describe two very different examples of the application of technology in New Zealand that illustrate some of the points I have been making. Both examples concern developments in transport fuels and resulted from the fact that the New Zealand economy was severely weakened by the two oil shocks of the 1970s.

In 1974, New Zealand imported nearly all its oil and oil products but had very large natural gas reserves. As a result of this situation, the use of CNG (compressed natural gas) as a transport fuel was developed. Today over 100,000 vehicles operate on CNG and some 450 refueling stations are in operation. This technology was very appropriate to New Zealand and could be developed and controlled on a local level.

The second oil shock arrived in 1979 and resulted in the building of the world's first gas-to-gasoline plant to produce about a third of New Zealand's gasoline. This development was a joint effort between the Mobil Oil Corporation and the New Zealand government and involved Mobil's technology. The plant was initially staffed primarily by secondees from Mobil Oil. However, as time has gone by, New Zealanders with the right educational background have been employed and trained. Today there are only a few Mobil secondees on site. This project is a good example of a country upgrading its technological capability through external assistance and the subsequent development of its educational system.

In summary, I believe that the application of technology in the Pacific islands can help economic development. However, technologies appropriate to one country may not be appropriate to another. Generally, I believe that a country should only introduce technology that it can control and maintain using local talent. A country can upgrade its technological capability through external assistance and by developing its educational system, particularly at secondary and tertiary levels. Also, for the innovative application of technology, entrepreneurial activity in the private sector must be encouraged through the creation of a climate of political and economic freedom. Finally, student mobility and the development and interaction of educational institutions in the region can be very powerful mechanisms to further technological, and hence, economic development in the Pacific islands.

Chapter 9

Technology and Development in the Asia-Pacific Region

Robert E. Driscoll

The economic development of the Asia-Pacific region has depended to a great extent on the success of the countries in the region in obtaining new and advanced technologies and in effectively applying them to increase production for domestic and international markets. Indeed, the hallmark of the Asia-Pacific region is its ready adoption of new technologies and new production processes. That the assimilation of technology has been successful is demonstrated by the fact that countries in the Asia-Pacific region are among the world's leaders in exports of a variety of sophisticated, technology intensive products.

Two major factors have contributed to the success of the Asia-Pacific region in assimilating new technologies: 1) an environment that encourages risk taking by private entrepreneurs; and 2) cooperation between government and industry in technology innovation and development.

Technology: an economic resource

To better understand the success of the Asia-Pacific region in adopting new technologies, it is important to understand technology and the factors that facilitate or impede its transfer. Technology is not a stagnant item; it is not a commodity that can be readily traded or that has an international fixed price. Technology is dynamic and changing; individuals and companies are continuously investing in new product developments, in better ways of producing goods and services, and in discovering new ways of meeting human needs. Thus, for the purposes of this paper, technology is defined as the knowledge necessary for an enterprise to function productively. Technology, therefore, includes process (engineering), management, marketing, and production know-how--in short, all aspects of a business, both intellectual and material.

Much has also been made of the "appropriateness" of technology, generally meaning technology applicable to small-scale or cottage industries. Many development experts contend that appropriate technology is the means by which developing countries can achieve self-sustaining economic advancement, the technologies applied by the Western countries being viewed as too capital intensive for the needs of most of the developing world.

Technology combines with traditional factors of production--land, labor, and capital--to allow a firm or a country to alter its normal comparative advantages. The appropriateness of the technology must therefore be measured in relation to its application. Certain high technologies, for example, may even be needed in the poorest countries if the country is to take advantage of a natural resource. Likewise, if the firm is aiming its production at supplying an international market, it must produce at a competitive price and quality. The selection of the technology to be employed, therefore, cannot be made from only one perspective; rather, market, natural resources, employment requirements, skill levels, and capital availability must be taken into account.

There is, therefore, no one appropriate technology for a particular country or for a given application. In certain instances, cost of labor may make it feasible to choose a technology that is less capital intensive. In other instances, the skill levels of the population may require more or less sophisticated production processes. The key issue is allowing the producer, no matter how poor a firm's surroundings, to be competitive with other producers who may have a more beneficial technological environment.

The transfer of commercial technology entails much more than the mere granting of a license to exploit a patent. It is a person-to-person process, involving the transfer of know-how, and the underlying knowledge of how to improve and adjust to changing conditions. Even when the technology is embodied in new equipment, there is technology involved in integrating the machine into an existing production line and in the training required for its operation, maintenance, and repair. This same commitment of seller and buyer is essential to successful transfer in services as well as in manufacturing sectors. Technology, in other words, cannot be transferred in a contractual agreement. The reaching of an agreement on the transfer of materials or methods is merely the beginning of the process of technology transfer.

Companies utilize a variety of techniques in transferring technology, including documentation, manuals, training materials, on-the-job and formal training, problem-solving assistance, technical visits, and seminars and workshops. These are made available over time and in accordance with the terms of the agreement between the buyer and the seller.

Perhaps the most important aspect of commercial technologies in our discussion is that its transfer cannot be dictated. Governments can place restrictions on the flow of technology. For example, U.S. export control laws are specifically designed to inhibit the transfer of sensitive technologies to the Soviet Union and Eastern bloc countries. Similarly, developing countries can limit their access to technologies by placing undue restrictions on the ability of companies to receive a fair value for the technology or to adequately protect it from unauthorized use.

Asia-Pacific policies attract technology

The countries in the Asia-Pacific region have been able to attract technologies needed for rapid economic expansion and industrial development. Several factors can be identified that have contributed to the willingness of firms to transfer their technologies into the region.

Reliance on the private sector

Throughout the Asia-Pacific region, the private sector is viewed as the principal engine of growth and economic expansion. While governments play a strong and decisive role in economic decision making, that role is generally one of setting the environment in which private firms are free to take risks.

Governments in the region, by and large, have established open economies that rely on market discipline to attract technology and capital. This same discipline forces companies to adapt to shifting market demands through the importation or development of new technologies.

In keeping with this reliance on the market and on the private sector, the countries of the Asia-Pacific region have enacted policies that encourage firms to search for and acquire modern technologies. While much has been made of the lack of intellectual property protection in the region (and this is indeed a critical problem), there are few restrictions on technology acquisition by private firms. These decisions are left to the marketplace, and governments do not attempt to micromanage technology acquisition.

What is most impressive throughout the region is the dynamic nature of the small- and medium-business sector. While there are large enterprises, entrepreneurs have consistently contributed more to employment generation and economic growth than these larger companies. While many may not be technologically sophisticated, these companies form the backbone of the economies of the Asia-Pacific region. Increasingly, these smaller firms are being relied upon by large companies and by foreign enterprises to supply ever more advanced components, providing the opportunity for smaller firms to improve their technical base. This interaction between large domestic and foreign firms and small entrepreneurial companies is an important element of the economic success of the region.

Stable economic and investment policies

The countries of the Asia-Pacific community have maintained consistent economic, fiscal, and monetary policies that have built confidence within the private sector to take risks through investment and technology transfer. Governments have therefore acted to set the stage upon which private companies can act flexibly and in response to changing market conditions and competitive opportunities. Singapore and Hong Kong are leading examples of countries that have aggressively and successfully sought foreign investment. That these countries have experienced a nearly unbroken record of economic growth can be traced to the confidence that foreign investors place in the continuity of their rules and regulations.

Even those countries that have placed some restrictions on foreign investment--limitations on foreign ownership in the case of Malaysia and the Philippines, for example--have not taken draconian measures that have undermined corporate confidence. There are exceptions written into the policies--one strong example being free trade zones that allow 100 percent foreign ownership. Those policies that do inhibit the flow of technology and new investments, such as intellectual property protection, are freely and openly debated and discussed with the private sector, and appropriate changes and improvements are being made.

What is most important is that the private sector knows and understands the rules of the game and can count on them to remain fundamentally the same. Where changes have been made, they have generally been designed to open the market further, and frequently result from free and open consultation with the private sector.

Successful transfer of technology must be made in an environment of confidence, both on the part of the foreign investor and the domestic private sector. The promise of regulatory consistency and of productive discussion and debate serves this purpose and lessens the likelihood that potential investors will be lost because of fear of mistreatment.

Policies on technology transfer

Over the past decade, there has been a great deal of debate concerning the importance of technological self-reliance. Development experts have encouraged countries to eschew the importation of modern Western technologies that have been developed around a set of factor endowments that do not necessarily reflect the needs of the developing countries. To a large extent, this debate corresponds to that on appropriate technology.

The most important goal of a producer is to achieve a level of productivity that allows him to compete with those who wish to capture the same markets. For most developing countries, this is accomplished most efficiently and cost effectively through the importation of already commercialized technologies.

Policies that inhibit that inflow dampen entrepreneurial innovation, limiting the markets that are open to a firm's products or services. It is only after a level of technological capability is achieved that the firm, and by inference the country, can afford the high cost of technology research and development (R & D).

Studies of science and technology policies and of the cycle of development of a domestic research and development capability indicate that the market is the critical variable calling forth productive R & D. Only as a market develops and matures, or is differentiated sufficiently, will firms create an R & D capability. Generally, that capability follows a progression of ever more sophisticated technical skills, beginning with quality control, and progressing through and including product and process adaptation and engineering.

No country can be completely dependent upon foreign technology. Therefore, expenditures on R & D and on stimulation of national innovative capabilities are essential to develop a scientific and technological orientation in the population. Likewise, no country is completely technologically independent. This is amply proven by the experiences of Japan and the United States. Japan, after World War II, imported technologies from the United States and Europe, relying on these transfers to help build a new industrial economy. Today, the United States and Europe are importing technology and production know-how from Japan.

Throughout the Asia-Pacific region firms have been free to identify technologies that are most applicable and appropriate to their needs and to acquire them on terms that are favorable to both buyer and seller. There is little, if any, review by governments of the terms of individual technology agreements. Government agencies allow the price and terms for a particular technology to be set by negotiation between buyer and seller. This is in clear contrast to the policies of many Latin American governments, which review individual contracts, often forcing companies to reduce the fees paid for technology. This may result in the firm acquiring what may be second-rate technology from a national source. Business plans may also be disrupted because the government has disallowed an agreement after the fact on the basis that a similar technology has already been acquired by another firm. These policies result in stifled corporate initiative.

While governments in the Asia-Pacific region do not interfere in corporate decision making, they provide important support to the process of technology acquisition and innovation. Once again, governments play a nurturing role, providing assistance through training, labor force development, financial grants for technical consultancies, and use of government commercial and trade offices to identify potential technology sources. Singapore clearly stands out in this regard, assisting companies to identify technology, investment, and trade opportunities through its Trade Development Board and Economic Development Board.

Problem areas

The most fundamental complaint of foreign investors regarding the Asia-Pacific region is the lack of intellectual property protection. Copyrights are infringed upon on a regular basis throughout the region, as are tradenames, trademarks, and patents.

Over the past several years, however, all of the countries in the Asia-Pacific region have been making progress in tightening their intellectual property laws as well as in effectively enforcing them. Nearly all the countries in the region are doing so because they believe they are succumbing to outside pressure. Singapore, the People's Republic of China, Indonesia, Malaysia, Thailand, and Taiwan have all enacted, or are enacting, new legislation to protect intellectual property. While it will take some time for the fears of certain investors to be overcome, these actions are clearly a signal that the countries of the Asia-Pacific region have taken note of the costs of past abuses.

A second factor that is often cited as an inhibitor to international investment and technology flows is that of market access. In several countries, specific sectors are reserved for national investors, either public or private. Investors in these sectors are also frequently limited to the national market, even though exports might be generated if new technologies were applied. A local investor may also be granted protections by the government that limits competition from import and from new investors. These protections amount to a refusal by governments to grant national treatment to foreign investors. Not only is the foreign investor hurt by this closure of market opportunities, but frequently the country remains behind international developments in technology, often resulting in a poorer quality and higher cost product for the domestic consumer. These problems differentially affect various industries, and their impacts must be assessed on a case by case basis. They are therefore problems that need to be considered by national governments seeking to increase investment and upgrade existing technologies.

A positive balance

Overall, the countries of the Asia-Pacific region have struck a positive balance in their treatment of foreign investment and technology. Their rules and regulations are stable and encourage risk taking by private investors. They attract the needed technologies because investors and technology suppliers can count on their own skills, not on the acts of governments alone, to ensure success or lead to failure in the marketplace.

Asia-Pacific nations can also boast of a close cooperation between industry and government in technology innovation and development. That cooperation is perhaps one of the most important factors that has enabled the countries of the region to assimilate advanced technologies so effectively.

Industry-government cooperation

Successful transfer and assimilation of technology depends both on the willingness of the source of the technology to transfer it to a given country and enterprise, and on the abilities of the user of the technology to effectively apply and assimilate it. Assimilation involves much more than merely utilizing a given technology efficiently; it also involves the ability of the company to identify new uses for technology and to identify new means of improving the productivity of the technology--in short, to begin its own, however limited, technology innovation.

Governments throughout the Asia-Pacific region have developed a number of innovative methods for assisting companies in technology assimilation. These programs have focused on private sector development by concentrating on two areas: 1) assistance in the immediate application of technology through development of user capabilities; and 2) assistance in technology innovation.

Three programs can be cited that have assisted companies in the selection of technology and in developing the necessary skills to apply and innovate technologies.

Training and labor force development

Several governments in the Asia-Pacific region have developed programs to assist companies in training and manpower development. One of the most attractive factors for investment in the Asia-Pacific region is the existence of an educated population, which allows for an easier transfer of technological know-how. Such programs further illustrate the commitment of the nations of the area to the development of an educated work force.

A noteworthy program to assist firms in their training needs is Singapore Skills Development Fund. SDF was created by the government of Singapore through a tax on employee wages. The fund provides cash assistance to companies for training and retraining employees, particularly for companies that are seeking to upgrade their technology and improve productivity.

In addition to assistance for training, SDF provides grants to companies for technical consultancies to determine how to improve productivity and to identify and install new technologies. By providing this assistance, the government of Singapore is able to stimulate the assimilation of new technologies by private firms without directing the firms as to which technologies they should adopt or which directions they should take to enhance productivity.

Nearly all Asia-Pacific countries have established productivity training centers that assist industry through training and consulting assistance to introduce new techniques to enhance productivity.

Another factor to be noted is the assistance provided by national standards agencies in improving quality control and in introducing new technologies for producing higher quality products. The Standards and Industrial Research Institute of Malaysia (SIRIM), for example, not only sets standards for a variety of products but also aids companies seeking to obtain the know-how to meet those standards.

Industry training centers

A number of industry-related training and technical assistance centers have been created through the joint efforts of foreign investors and governments. IBM, for example, has established a software institute in Singapore with the National University of Singapore. They have also assisted in the creation of a regional computer center at the Asian Institute of Technology in Bangkok. This center is now involved in developing a computer-aided-design and computer-aided-manufacturing capability to provide product design and manufacturing assistance to private firms.

Industry training and technical assistance centers provide a wealth of practical know-how and experience that the private sector can draw upon in implementing their own technology modernization strategies. They have the added benefit of strong support from individual companies or from industry groups. This ensures that they are able to keep pace with new technical innovations.

Information access

Selection of the appropriate technology requires access to information on technology alternatives as well as on new developments in the marketplace. This is another area in which governments can and have assisted the private sector. The governments of developed countries have also provided assistance through grants to specialized agencies whose mission is to enhance access to commercial and technical information.

The U.S.-ASEAN Center for Technology Exchange is a relatively new organization that is supported by the U.S. government and by U.S. corporations. The U.S.-ASEAN center provides a variety of programs that help companies to better understand technology alternatives, to learn about new technologies and their application in new situations, and to identify sources of technology and technical assistance in the United States. Its technical seminars on a variety of industry topics are specifically oriented toward senior managers who are faced with making strategic decisions regarding the future of their companies and with assessing their technology alternatives. The missions to the United States that are sponsored by the center are specifically aimed at helping companies in the ASEAN region to learn firsthand how a technology is applied by a firm in the United States and to learn about new productivity and production management programs employed by U.S. firms. They also enable ASEAN managers to meet with U.S. firms interested in discussing technology tie-ups, technical assistance agreements, and joint ventures.

The Japanese government has supported similar programs. One institution that offers such programs in ASEAN is the Technology Transfer Institute (TTI), which is based in Singapore. TTI's programs include industry-specific seminars in ASEAN and missions to Japan. JETRO and the Ministry of International Trade and Industry have also sponsored these types of programs in ASEAN and throughout Asia.

Technonet Asia, which operates through its national participating organizations, provides assistance to companies through its technical seminars and by making available experts that consult with a number of companies on their technology and productivity needs. Technonet relies on individuals with specialized expertise in a particular industry or technology to conduct hands-on training programs of several weeks in duration. These programs are important in helping a firm to become familiar with a technology, with means of improving productivity, or with ways of changing the applications of a particular technology or piece of equipment.

These programs also assist companies in identifying their own technology needs, as well as the alternative technologies and transfer means available to them. Since these programs are aimed principally at smaller enterprises, they focus on technology exchange programs that can be implemented with limited resources. These services are important in helping a firm to develop problem solving, technology evaluation, and installation and utilization capabilities. Technonet is supported by grants from the United States, Canada and Japan as well as through fees generated from participating companies.

Other organizations that companies can call upon for assistance in technology assimilation and problem solving are the various national executive service corps. The U.S. International Executive Services Corps, founded in the 1960s, has sent retired executives to individual firms to assist them with particular technical or managerial problems. Japan and several European countries have developed similar programs.

Technology innovation

The above efforts to provide assistance to firms in identifying a particular technology, in labor force development, and in technology assimilation are supplemented by government programs aimed at technology innovation and development. Several programs are in place throughout Asia and have been particularly successful in helping companies move beyond dependence on foreign technologies toward independent innovation and new product development and commercialization.

The Korean Advanced Institute of Science and Technology (KAIST) is perhaps one of the best known institutions of its kind in Asia. KAIST was organized by the Korean government to be the premiere research and development institute for the country. From the beginning, however, it has been required that KAIST work closely with the private sector. Indeed, the Korean government does not provide full funding for KAIST; the institute must sell its services to private companies in order to meet its annual budget.

This close cooperation between industry- and government-sponsored institutions helps assure that the efforts of R & D activity have relevance to the needs of industry and have a commercial and economic value to the country. Whereas basic research is not fully excluded, the application of that research to national problems is emphasized.

Cooperative research partnerships have been established between the United States, India, and Israel. These cooperative agreements are designed to assist U.S. and national firms in entering into agreements on technology sharing and technology development. Generally drawing on small- and medium-sized U.S. companies, the alliances established through these cooperative programs facilitate technology development and adaptation in the host country while opening new markets for both U.S. and national firms.

These latter programs are in their early stages of implementation. The program in Israel, however, has already formed over 100 joint development efforts between U.S. and Israeli corporations.

Other efforts in the region include the formation of the Thailand Science and Technology Development Program, which is supported by the Thai government and the U.S. Agency for International Development. This science and technology (S & T) program is intended to help establish a commercial R & D capability in Thailand, while at the same time helping Thai businessmen to make better decisions on the selection and acquisition of current commercial technologies. This linkage of transfer and development, coupled with a built-in commercial orientation of the R & D centers, is a unique and experimental feature of this project.

Perhaps the one area that remains lacking in the science and technology realm is that of a close tie between the productive community and the university research centers. This lack of cooperation limits the ability of universities to contribute to national technology development, because researchers do not have practical knowledge of the needs of the business community. It further inhibits the private sector, because the firm must either develop an R & D capability itself or continue to look to international sources for new technical advancements. The Thai S & T project is a step toward building bridges between university research centers and the business community. Several activities of the National University of Singapore, including the software institute, are also attempting to build these linkages, but there is clearly more that must be done to improve this type of cooperation.

Lessons for the future

Technology has contributed substantially to the transformation of the economies of the Asia-Pacific region. That transformation has encompassed a shift in the economies of the region from being primary commodity suppliers to being major producers of internationally traded goods and services. From high-technology electronic products to light consumer goods, the Asia-Pacific nations have aggressively sought out and effectively applied new technologies.

The success of the region is owed, in large measure, to an environment that encourages risk taking by private businessmen. This environment is reflected in government policies that attract new capital investments from foreign and domestic enterprises, an open trading system that mandates that businessmen produce goods and services that meet international price and quality standards, and government programs and policies that stimulate and assist firms in the acquisition and application of new technologies. The necessity of creating a nurturing environment, rather than one in which overregulation hampers the growth of opportunity, becomes especially apparent when one looks at the success of the Asia-Pacific region and the failures elsewhere in the transfer and assimilation of technology.

Role of industry

Foreign enterprises have played a significant role in the transformation of the region. Their investments here have brought new technologies and new employment opportunities. These enterprises have contributed substantially through internal training programs and through technical assistance and training for suppliers and customers. This has helped in developing a broader industrial base in the region.

Equally important is the new capital brought into the region through direct investments and joint ventures as well as the markets that have been opened for manufactured products. This opening of new markets has facilitated the move by domestic producers to acquire new technologies and, subsequently, to improve product quality and become more competitive in international markets.

Domestic firms have helped stimulate the extensive growth of the domestic markets, including the development of new products and the development of new uses for the region's natural resources. Domestic firms have relied on underlying comparative advantages to become suppliers to the international markets as well. Much of this growth is based on the ability of these firms to acquire and apply new technologies.

The dynamic interaction between industry and government in technology acquisition and assimilation has been instrumental in the success of the countries of the region in transforming their economies. Countries that are seeking to build a broader economic base should look carefully at the experiences of the Asia-Pacific region, particularly in terms of the roles that industry and government have played in the technological modernization of the region.

Chapter 10

The Role of Technology: A South Pacific Islander's Perspective

Tau'ili'ili Uili Meredith

Introduction

Dr. Arthur T. Mosher of the Agriculture Development Council based in New York defines technology "as simply how we do things,"[1] or the know-how of doing things. A dictionary definition of technology is "the systematic application of knowledge to practical tasks in industry." At the outset, I wish to make the point that we make and do things correctly most of the time, but sometimes we do things wrong. This applies to the right and, if you like, the wrong technology.

Oftentimes the technology is well-intended but may be inappropriate to the situation in which it is to be applied for many reasons, including those based on the levels of technology, economics, and environment, as well as on the levels of training and understanding and incompatibility with social and traditional systems, which I consider an important consideration. Overall it is owing to a lack in communications, particularly those that should occur between the inventors of technologies, their transferers, and their ultimate users. Moreover, a control on the adaptation of technologies is important, particularly where the application is to have effects at the national level.

Within this South Pacific region, the expressions of "appropriate technology" and "technological innovations and their transfer" are used quite frequently, even in situations where English is not a first language. There is also a general acceptance, if not submissively so, in this day and age of the multiplicity in technologies, that somewhere out there, there is a huge transformational resource in technology. Transformational, however, in the sense that, to use an expression from the marital vow, they could transform "for better or for worse." Frankly, this resource can be quite frightening.

History is full of useful technologies, and technological changes have profoundly affected society as exemplified by those that have freed humanity from slavery, such as labor-saving technologies, and the printing press that freed the human mind.

Aid is a common vehicle for technology transfer. In a recent UNESCO publication,[2] reference was made to an inappropriate technology, in fact a technology that misfired. In some atolls, islanders have used drop toilets placed over the lagoons where they also wash and fish. A team of foreign experts flew in to teach them to dig pit toilets on land and then departed. Months later, people became sick and died of cholera as pollution fed into the fresh water underlying the small land area, which was the only source of fresh water. A new team of foreign experts then flew in, threw their hands up in horror, and told the people to go back to traditional methods. Since these "experts" were from the developed West, they did not tell the islanders about the composting type of toilet. In another case, flush toilets provided free by an aid team were blocked by leaves just weeks after the aid team had left, islanders naturally not being aware of the limitations of such modern devices.

These cases, one hopes, are isolated. But they serve to illustrate that clearly at least two parties should talk over and understand the technology--the technology transferers and the users. What is "appropriate" must be viewed from two sides. Little is learned from the past when one fails to ask, "Why has current practice persisted from the past?" and when one fails to follow up early enough on the induced technology to be sure that it is fulfilling its desired aim.

Technological changes find their base in a wide range of mainly scientific disciplines, although the social sciences form a base that is regarded as quite important in the South Pacific. Most certainly social science-based considerations receive priority for the South Pacific region in the application of technology, if not in its origin. It is the selection of technological packages and the management of them that is of paramount importance.

Sometimes in global technological advancements, such as the revolution in communication through television and telecommunications, we, as a people, enjoy the effects of bringing the world's people together with, and often without, comprehension.

Technological changes based on studies in the life sciences represent a category that, because of the economic importance of agriculture and of food production in our region, will translate relevantly to South Pacific islands. However, a warning has been set off of a possible global movement in handing over the role of farmers to the control of scientists. I will deal with this subject later.

Knowledge is the ultimate source of technology, and wisdom must prevail in its application.

The setting

I applaud the decision of the Global Community Forum to focus on the theme, "Pacific Cooperation and Development," and especially the choice of the venue. Exposure to conditions in Apia and Western Samoa will provide additional insight into the setting of the South Pacific Basin island countries. Our obvious geographic features are our smallness, isolation, physical fragmentation, and associated problems characteristic of less-developed countries, problems that tend to be more acute in our region--our increasing dependence, our very small population, the lack of diversification in exports, disproportionately underdeveloped industrial sectors, and so on.[3]

The South Pacific basin countries and technology

The important characteristics of this region that are more pertinent to a forum session on technology are: the limited range of a trained labor force and skills, especially in science; the relative lack of training facilities; the disparity that exists between the trained technologists and the users of the technologies, usually rural dwellers, traditionally conservative and tradition-steeped societies; the fragility of our ecosystems with associated tradition-based taboos; and the primary occupation of the South Pacific people with agriculture (including fisheries, stock, and forestry), with food production, and with traditional food preparation.

One other characteristic that has an important bearing on our region with reference to technology is the diversity of foreign powers that have administered some of the island groups (some are still tenaciously hanging on!) and the flow of transferred technology from the metropolitan powers to their respective colonies or to their former colonies. Such trends are still evident today, as exemplified by the sugar cane industry of Fiji, and the use and promotion of certain French breeds of cattle in Vanuatu and New Caledonia and their associated animal husbandry practices. This is equally reflected in other nonagricultural fields, such as in medical science, in the systems of government, in education, and even in the make of vehicles and the left- or right-hand driving rules observed by road travelers in every form of transportation.

On a global level, agrotechnology transfer, based on similar soil and climate conditions for certain crops and crop combinations, makes it possible to pass on those crops and crop husbandry practices. For such transfers, a world classification of soils has to be "mapped." But it appears that this is not possible because the FAO, the Americans, and the French, to name the major parties involved, could not come to an agreed-upon world soil classification system.

Closer to home and confined to a division of whole islands, Eastern Samoa appears to have metamorphosized its societies with the help of U.S.

technologies. This is in contrast with the Western part that is independent and appears to have had and to currently have a totally different attitude, not so much to ward adopting selected technologies per se, but toward examining the effects, including the side effects, in the light of our culture. Both Samoas have had mixed results from their experience.

In extreme conditions, such as those prevalent in atoll islands of coralline soils, high pH, sea and salt contamination, and more fragile ecosystems, traditional taboos are observed. Such prohibitions might be analyzed, and if worth sharing with other similar atoll island groups, might be carefully and cautiously transferred.

Similarly, an inventory of tradition-based technologies might be a useful first move, followed by a sharing of them in compatible situations--compatible mainly on sociological grounds. In fact, in a region relatively advanced in the organization of their societies, it behooves us all to examine science-based technologies for compatibility with social science-based factors. To overcome the claim of disparity between technologists and the users of technology, such an examination would be more effectively done between users of technologies and potential users. That is, if it is a farming technology, farmers practicing it could be more effective in transferring it.

Agronomically, the growing of rice is feasible in Samoa. We import rice and could at least grow it to substitute for the imported rice, even if we are not inclined to export it. But rice growing does not suit the "climate of the people" here. In other words, the technology of rice growing here makes it feasible, and perhaps economically so, but it is incompatible with the social make-up of our people.

The equalization of the opportunity to spread what might be regarded as appropriate technology has been effected through regional organizations such as the South Pacific Commission (S. P. C.), and the South Pacific Bureau of Economic Cooperation (S. P. E. C.) within the region, and perhaps more recently through the United Nations and its specialized agencies. A summary view on the South Pacific Basin countries and technology is quoted below from a report presented to the UN Conference on Science and Technology for Development, following a seminar in the South Pacific:

> Our development so far has widened the gap between our tradition and modern sectors and our rural and urban communities. Because of our greater dependence on externally generated technology, we are vulnerable to economic domination by foreign suppliers and fluctuations in the world economy. Our small number of export commodities, and few local professionals (increasing vulnerability to brain drain) will lead us to far greater disparity than most less developed countries, at the mercy of the more powerful nations and organizations.[4]

One such foreign powerful nation has been attracted to this region, allegedly in response to a call to fill a need in fisheries technology!

But the Pacific aspires to peace, to conservation of not only its traditions but its resources in terms of land and sea, and especially its people. Pacific basin countries have declared development goals that are consistent with conventions. These goals are a secured and respected national sovereignty and independence all around, and to be freedom from inequalities, unemployment, and poverty. Above all, we aspire to remain the happy people we are, securing the same freedom our forefathers had for our succeeding generations of the future. We, in our turn, wish to maintain, even improve on, the heritage we pass on to those who succeed us. We want therefore the technology packages that would attain these basic goals for development.

Technology-based resources in the South Pacific

Resources of technology are those inherent from our tradition and culture, those adopted as introduced from past colonial administration and those more recently introduced. A tentative listing reveals the following institutions with involvements in technology:

1. The University of Technology in Lae and the University of Papua New Guinea in Papua New Guinea;
2. The regional University of the South Pacific and the Fiji Institute of Technology in Fiji;
3. Education Ministries of South Pacific Basin countries at training levels in the primary, secondary, and in some cases at the tertiary levels in technical training. Such would include the Solomon Islands' College of Higher Education with specialized schools in agriculture, home science and trades training; the Navuso Farming Institute and the Lololo Forestry College in Fiji, and so on;
4. Community Colleges in former trust territories of the United States;
5. The American Samoa Community College, closer to home, has instructional programs that include technology. The recent introduction of computerization at the American Samoa Community College in the region the French IHRO, its coconut-based research work in French Polynesia and in Vanuatu, and its oceanographic arm, the ORSTOM in New Caledonia, have made contributions to a technology in the region; and
6. Mention is made of the potential to be tapped of the resource base at the Asian Institute of Technology.

What kind of technology for the Pacific basin countries?

One decision that has already been made by government leaders of Pacific Basin countries involves high technology (high-tech) at PICHTR, mentioned earlier, which was established in 1983. The decision was made in August 1984 to do research on open-cycle ocean thermal energy conversion (OC-OTEC). OC-OTEC holds great potential as a source of energy for electricity, fresh drinking water, air conditioning, and aquaculture. OC-OTEC is part of PICHTR but based in Hawaii. The ocean-based high-tech research is a logical follow up to the Exclusive Economic Zone that placed large parts of the ocean under the jurisdiction of many island nations in the Pacific basin. PICHTR is researching energy systems for isolated regions, that is, alternative energy research that includes wind-, geothermal- and solar-based generators or energy. The Japanese government has formed a partnership with PICHTR.[5] PITCHR main divisions of labor are in energy and resources technology, information technology, biotechnology, and education and international relations.[6] Interest must be maintained on the progress of PICHTR.

UNESCO has proposed a program on management of science and technology for development of the Pacific following a three-man mission in late 1985. A UNESCO-SPEC high-level regional meeting on policy and management of science and technology in development in the South Pacific region was held in Apia earlier this year. In the absence of an accessible record of the outcome of that meeting, some reservations must be made on its potential and possible effects in the creation of technology and its application.

Technology, given the disparity in the levels of training of national scientists and the users of it, must be researched as closely as possible to home. World scientists would be at even greater disparity. In any event, training is required to afford understanding of technology at all levels.

Perhaps, in the realization of the potential of technology as a transformational resource, we might consider this potential in terms of transitional levels of training, or translational phases, from the inventors to the ultimate users.

With a declared bias, I venture to suggest that, considering the importance of agriculture to the region, technologies that improve primary industries (agriculture, stock, fisheries, and forestry) ought to be given priority consideration. It could be presented that rural development is the same as the development of the primary industries in the Pacific basin countries. For egalitarian reasons, economic development is rural development and the development of the majority of the people.

In a region comparatively free of the ravages of war, of food shortages, not to mention famine, and of major plagues, the issue of food security has been hinted at and is surfacing now as a challenge, perhaps more from the drive to reverse the domination of imports in trade and trade balances.

In respect to technology, the South Pacific has benefitted from the advancements made in crop breeding. For instance, head cabbages were not produced in the hotter part of our region until commercially affordable so-called tropicalized seed from the Japan-based Takii Seed Company became available. Head cabbage production is now a matter of course. Tomato growing used to be limited during the more humid rainy seasons until the Asian Vegetable Research and Development Center supported by, among other donors, the Asian Development Bank, bred and made available its variety called Hot Days and Hot Nights--a particular variety that responds well to a low diurnal temperature variation. Tomato production is now possible year round. Seed packaging is a very transferable technology. Perhaps the Green Revolution, with its celebrated successes in wheat and rice, has not benefitted us directly. Indirectly, it has. While on the whole plant-breeding technologies have been of benefit to us, the caution I raised earlier has to do with the high technology of plant genetic engineering.

Crop varieties are now being developed that are less pesticide- and fertilizer-dependent. The introduction of earlier Green Revolution crops displaced the cultivation of traditional varieties in many areas of the Third World. Today, many of these traditional varieties and their priceless genetic variation are disappearing, forcing some Third World agricultural economies increasingly in the direction of Green Revolution monoculture.

Ironically, in displacing traditional agriculture, the Green Revolution displaced the very genetic variability that once worked to resist crop disease and insect infestation. Without pesticides, the early Green Revolution crop varieties, though high-yielding in favorable circumstances, were often vulnerable to considerable insect damage. This initial shortcoming sent Green Revolution plant breeders on a catch-up program of plant breeding for disease resistance that continues today.

We are at the beginning of an unprecedented revolution in the food industry. The rapid development of genetic engineering and biotechnology is changing the practice of agriculture and food manufacture, moving control from farmers to scientists, and even more significantly, to those who own the technology. The book *Altered Harvest*, by Jack Doyle,[7] traces this transformation. It is about the race to own the biological and genetic ingredients of agriculture and thus the control of "food power" in the world markets:

> The United States is on the leading edge of a powerful new era in food making--an era in which all agriculture and much of food manufacturing will be reshaped by genetic technology, by gene splicing in crops, embryo engineering in livestock and powerful new microchemicals that will turn-on the genes of entire fields of wheat, potatoes, etc.
> Food will be more finely shaped at its point of origin at the level of the seed, the gene and the molecule. Food will begin in the laboratory rather than the farmer's field. Crops will still be

grown in the fields, but they will be given their biological marching orders by scientists who design them in the laboratory.

It is theoretically possible for the technology to be applied, and for it to improve food production, environmental quality, and agricultural diversity. The immediate concern is to make sure these values are protected. But the risks will be ever present.

Because biotechnology and "super-genetics" are prone to takeover by the multinational corporations, there is a major power shift taking place that is moving control of food away from those who grow it. Farmers are heading for a new kind of dependence. This will reduce their options and diminish livestock and crop diversity.

Much of the promised technology appears potentially good and benign. Doyle wrote of "pesticide-free" agriculture, self-fertilizing crops, and nutritionally produced food--of abundant harvest, even in the most arid regions. But he warns of serious concerns--concerns about how the new technology will affect food security, environmental quality, and biological diversity. The genetic manipulation of crops, farm animals, chemicals, and micro-organisms will not be without risk. "One very persistent microbe or errant gene that wrongly colonizes an important ecological niche could touch off a chain reaction of ecological and political events" that could disrupt a country's food supply.

Technology research on biological nitrogen, such as the programs of the Australian Center for International Agricultural Research (ACIAR), would find application in this region. So too would the replenishing and restocking of clams now depleted from our seas as carried out by the ACIAR, in close collaboration with the James Cook University in Townsville. A linkage with the National University of Samoa's proposed research program and the marine science research of the James Cook University will be explored and would hold considerable potential for this region also.

The needs to maintain and to improve the quality of life in the South Pacific basin require a balanced approach to the introduction of technology. Dependence of this region on the major powers for the prevention of technologies that adversely affect our limited environment is put forward as a plea to this forum.

Notes

1. A. T. Mosher, A. D. C., "Getting Agriculture Moving," (1970).
2. J. C. Robinson, "Interaction between Culture and Economic Development in the South Pacific," UNESCO.
3. R. G. Ward and A. Procto, "South Pacific Agriculture: Choices and Constraints," 1980 (ADB/ANU).

4. Rothman et al., "The South Pacific Sub-Regional Seminar on Science and Technology" report to the UNSTD (1958).
5. PICHTR News, vol. 2, (Winter, 1986).
6. PICHTR Annual Report, (1986).
7. Jack Doyle, *Altered Harvest* (New York: Viking). Reviewed in *Pacific World: An International Quarterly on Peace and Ecojustice* 3, (May, 1987).

Chapter 11

A Marine Ranch Concept Using a Sunflower ("Himawari")

Kei Mori

Introduction

The development of "marine ranches" is based on the idea of allowing fish to "graze." In many existing fish culture farms, fish are confined within a very small enclosed area and fed from shore. This is unhealthy for the fish and the environment in many ways. The residual (uneaten) food settles to the sea bottom and can lead to the creation of sulfur gas. Furthermore, because these fish farms are frequently overcrowded, large numbers of fish often become sick. To remedy this, the fish are usually fed large quantities of medicine, much of which can remain unprocessed in fish bodies and can affect the people who eventually eat them. This type of fish culture farm is causing many problems in Japan. Other fish culture farms are being developed in which fish are confined within a large area, and are conditioned to come to shore periodically by means of a sound-producing device. Although this eliminates the overcrowding problem, there is still the danger of large amounts of natural pollution in the form of residual food and fish droppings.

The purpose of the marine ranch is to create a favorable environment to attract fish, rather than to confine them within an enclosed area. The proposed marine ranch eliminates many of the undesirable characteristics of present day fish farms and is healthier for both the fish and for the environment. Food is not put into the water but is *recycled* from overnourished water. In the process of recycling food, these marine ranches also help to eliminate oxygen-deficient water masses that often form in the lower strata during the summer months.

Marine ranches can incorporate underwater corridors from which tourists can observe fish in their natural habitat. In the marine ranches, chlorella will be cultivated in underwater tanks that are irradiated with value-added solar rays. Light will also be irradiated *around* the tanks, to encourage plankton growth and to allow people to see the fish, which are attracted to the light.

The marine ranch will also be useful in growing coral. The plankton that grows on coral requires large amounts of sunlight for its photosynthetic process and therefore generally grows only in very clear water. By bringing sunlight to the lower levels of the sea, the Sunflower marine ranch can indirectly foster coral growth in these areas.

It is clear that the marine ranch will be beneficial in many ways. In summary, it will:

1. increase the productivity of fishing grounds;
2. help to purify sea water;
3. create an excellent tourist attraction as well as research facilities; and
4. foster coral growth where previously it was not possible.

Modular structure of the Sunflower marine ranch and its construction process

The writer proposes a marine ranch module composed of seven systems. Each system consists of seven "19-eye" Sunflower units with an effective light-receiving area of 1.5 square meters each. (Such a system was exhibited at the Tsukuba International Scientific Fair, Government Theme Pavilion A.) The module has a diameter of 80 meter, and covers an area of about 5,000 square meters. It can be used in conjunction with other modules and can be installed along any coast.

Each module has a number of underwater observation corridors, which are arranged in a honeycomb pattern. The corridors lie 10 meters below the surface of the sea at the bottom of the coastal euphotic layer. The photosynethetic chlorella culture tanks are hung from the corridors. A total of 21 chlorella culture tanks are attached to each module. At least two out of each cluster of seven 19-eye Sunflowers are used to supply the value-added solar rays to each culture tank and its periphery. Each Sunflower system has 7 Sunflowers and is set on a hexagonal steel tower station that has a diameter of 3 meter and rises 10 meters above the surface of the sea. The station allows for a 3 meter range of the tide and is based on a 20 meter-high submarine hexagonal steel tower having a diameter of 6 meters. This steel tower station is designed to withstand typhoons; it can weather winds of 90 meters per second and waves of up to 14 meters (with an 8 meter peak and a 6 meter trough). The probable impact upon each station (6 tons per square meter) is designed to be dispersed by the honeycomb-like pattern of the corridors. The only areas where the force is concentrated are the joints between the station and its observation corridors. Hence if a mechanism to absorb the impact force is installed there, there is no problem.

The proposed module is designed to be as large as possible, but small enough to be constructed on a large shipway and transported via ocean-going vessel (see Figures 11.1 and 11.2). Thus it can be built in any shipyard and installed at any coast. It can be sunk into the water by ballasting and fastened to a preconstructed base. The module is designed to be installed off the Okinawa coast, an area that sees strong typhoons every summer. Its intended service life is 30 years, which includes a spare-parts supply for 15 years.

Figure 11.1.
Cross section of the Sunflower's modular structure.

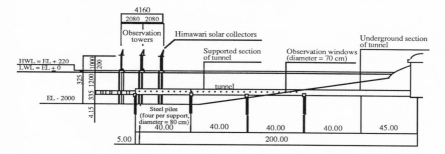

Figure 11.2.
Top view of Sunflower's modular structure.

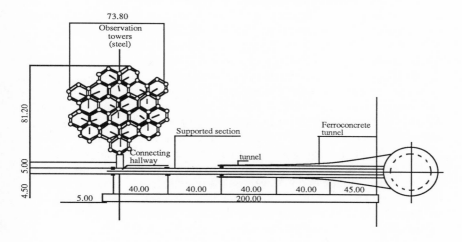

The module can be expanded by adding one or two joints to each corridor as illustrated in Figure 11.3.

Figure 11.3
Enlarged view of Sunflower's modular structure

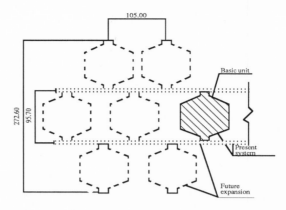

The formation mechanism of the Sunflower marine ranch

The Sunflower marine ranch would *create* food by taking nutrients from the overnourished lower stratum of the sea and by fostering the growth of chlorella algae. To understand this process, it is first necessary to understand the normal behavior of sea water.

The behavior of sea water varies with the tidal currents and with the seasons; the variation in temperature between summer and winter causes the relatively warm bottom water to intermix via convection.. This causes nutrient salts to ascend from the bottom to the surface, which in turn allows photosynthesis to advance. No oxygen deficient water is generated.

In autumn and spring, strong winds agitate and mix the sea water. Unfortunately, this is not the case in summer. In the summer, intensified solar radiation and higher atmospheric temperature increase the temperature of the surface water, creating a larger temperature differential between the surface water and the water underneath. Consequently, the water becomes stratefied in fixed surface and bottom layers. From May to June of every year, photosynthesis occurs in the surface layer, consuming many of the nutrient salts. The result is a shortage of nutrient salts, and even an ample supply of solar energy available in July and August can not help advance the photosynthesis. In the bottom layer, on the other hand, the water temperature does not rise at all. The light from above does not reach it, and the water is not intermixed with water from above; the overnutrition worsens the oxygen-deficient condition, and no photosynthesis takes place.

As a result of this oxygen-deficient condition in the overnourished bottom-layer sea water, metals from the sea bottom are dissolved. When these minerals reach a certain concentration, sudden abnormal breeding of poisonous vegetable plankton occurs. Sometimes they cover the entire surface of the sea. The aforementioned process is said to be responsible for the proliferation of noxious plankton, such as those that cause red tides.

Even without any abnormal development of plankton, the oxygen deficient water masses formed in the bottom layer create an inhospitable environment. In the Ohmura Bay of Kyushu Island, often large numbers of fish are forced ashore by the oxygen-deficient water flooding the bay before a typhoon. Occasionally, fish suddenly disappear from the bay.

The Sunflower marine ranch would help to alleviate the stratification problem and create food for fish in the following way: oxygen-deficient but overnourished water (water rich in nitrogen and phosphorus) is fed from the bottom layer into the culture tanks and irradiated with value-added solar rays (consisting primarily of visible solar radiation--ultraviolet, heat, and two-thirds of the infrared radiation are filtered out). This is supplied continuously by the optical radiator.[1]   Thus the chlorella photosynthesizes and multiplies at an advanced rate. When the volume of dissolved oxygen reaches a certain level, the oxygenized water and cholorella are discharged from the tank. Overnourished, oxygen-deficient water is simultaneously fed into the tank, and chlorella continue to photosynthesize and proliferate.

In this cycle, nitrogen and phosphorus are recovered from the sea. At the same time, dissolved oxygen, chlorella, and other useful phytoplankton are discharged into the sea. Chlorella are then eaten by rotifer (zooplankton) which are a favorite food of fry and fingerlings. Fry and fingerlings are in turn eaten by medium- and large-sized fish in the food chain. This is the process by which the marine ranch makes for prolific fishing grounds.

The green light emitted from the chlorella culture tank attracts a number of various migratory fish. To allow phytoplankton, which float near the culture tank when discharged, to continue to photosynthesize, the value-added solar radiation is irradiated both into the tank and around it. The solar radiation helps to maintain the health of the fish and to foster a good general ocean environment. Scrapped ships could be sunk near the tanks as artificial reefs, or a fishing net composed of laser and optical fibers could be installed to catch fish and to allow observation of their health and growing conditions.

Productivity of the marine ranch

The area covered by each module is about 5,000 square meters, and the effective light-condensing area per module is 75.5 square meters, or one-seventieth of the coverage. The volume is equivalent to 50,000 cubic meters each for the surface stratum (0 to 10 meters deep) and for the bottom stratum (10 to 20 meters deep). The productivity of chlorella per day, as estimated from the productivity of an open pool system, is 3.0×10^{15} units, or 18.75 kilograms (dry weight), for the surface layer production, and $2.94 \text{ s } 10^{14}$ units, or 1.85 kilograms, for the bottom-layer production. A simulation based on these data was done to determine chlorella mass production rates in the bottom layer (see Table 11.1). The overall productivity of a marine ranch based on these estimates is summarized in Table 11.2. The results shown in Tables 11.1 and 11.2 were used to estimate the absorption of N and P in the bottom layer (Table 11.3) and the increase of dissolved oxygen in the bottom layer (Table 11.4).

Table 11.1
Simulation to determine chlorella mass production rates
in bottom layer
(10 m to 20 m Deep)

Description	October Conditions experimental data[1]	Case I effect of sea temperature[2]	Case II effect of light intensity[3]	Case III combined effect of case and case II[4]
Chlorella production [cells/day]	2.94×10^{14} (1)	4.59×10^{14} ((1)x1.56)	4.03×10^{14} ((1)x1.37)	6.29×10^{14} ((1)x1.56x 1.37)
Sea Temperature [degrees C]	20 (Oct. mean)	25 (Aug. mean)	20 (Oct. mean)	25 (Aug. mean)
Light intensity [MJ/m2]	13.6 (Oct. mean)	13.6 (Oct. mean)	18.6 (Oct. mean)	18.6 (Oct. mean)
Method of calculating Chlorella algae biomass production per day		growth change rates: at 20 C: 1.07% 1/h at 25 C: 1.09 % 1/h $1.07^{24} = 5.07$ $1.09^{24} = 7.91$ 7.91 5.07 divided by = 1.56	18.6-13.6 divided by = 1.37	(case I)x(case II) = 2.14

1. Experiment was conducted at the Nagasaki Prefectural Culture Laboratory at Nobosaki.
2. Temperature is increased to 25 C from 20 C, temperature in October (base case). All other conditions remain the same.
3. Amount of light per day is increased to 18.6 MJ/m^2 from 13.6 MJ/m^2 (base case). All other conditions remain the same.
4. Temperature is increased to 25 C and amount of light per day is increased to 18.6 MJ/m^2.

Table 11.2
The overall productivity of a marine ranch

Productivity per day		October Conditions	Sunflower biomass production in the bottom layer (10 m to 20 m deep)			Factors for food chain calculation
			Case I	Case II	Case III	
Chlorella	quantity of chlorella (cells)	2.94×10^{14}	4.59×10^{14}	4.03×10^{14}	6.29×10^{14}	number of chlorella cells per 1 g chlorella (dry weight) 1.59×10^{11} cells 6.29×10^{-12} g/cells
	dry weight [kg]	1.85	2.89	2.53	3.96	
Rotifer: zoo plankton (Brachionus plicatilis [Wamushi in Japanese]) [cells]		1.84×10^{9}	2.87×10^{9}	2.52×10^{9}	3.93×10^{9}	number of chlorella needed for a rotifer 1.60×10^{5} cells
Sea-bream fry (size: 6 mm) [number of fish]		5.27×10^{6}	8.22×10^{6}	7.22×10^{6}	11.26×10^{6}	number of rotifer needed for one sea-bream fry 3.49×10^{2} cells
Black sea-bream fry (size: 6 mm) [number of fish]		3.21×10^{6}	5.00×10^{6}	4.39×10^{6}	6.85×10^{6}	number of rotifer needed for one black sea-bream 5.74×10^{2} cells

Table 11.3
Simulation model for dissolved oxygen (DO) increase in the bottom layer (10 m to 20 m deep) using SUNFLOWER

DO setup standard	Range of DO increase value	Required days to increase DO testing			
		October	Case I	Case II	Case III
Oxygen deficient	0 ppm	128 days	82 days	94 days	60 days
	5 ppm				
Fishery class 2[1] Fishing environment Water quality standard (sea under environmental standards	5 ppm	26 days	16 days	19 days	12 days
	6 ppm (or more)				
Fishery class 1[2] (Sea under environmental standards)	6.0 ppm	38 days	25 days	28 days	18 days
	7.5 ppm (or more)				

1 Fishery class 2--for marine products such as mullets, sea weed, etc.
2 Fishery class 1--for marine products such as porgies, yellow-tails, undaria, etc., including those of Class 2.

Conclusion

It is clear that the volume of dissolved oxygen produced by the proliferation of phytoplankton in the sea's bottom layer would be sufficient to multiply the breeding of fry. Based on the aforementioned assessment of feasibility of the marine ranch formation, the possibilities of sea water decontamination through nitrogen/phosphorous recovery and of oxygen supply using vegetable plankton have been suggested. It has also been suggested that it could be used as a marine tourist attraction. The modular structure was designed to withstand billows and surges; its safety could be verified by a small-scale model.

The development and construction of a marine ranch of this kind would definitely help to maintain fishing grounds without interfering with or disturbing the peaceful lifestyle of fishers. It apparently would be easy to solicit local public support for such projects.

Table 11.4
Absorption (removal) of N and P in bottom layer
(10 m to 20 m deep) using SUNFLOWER 4

| | Simulation | | Required for Days of Absorption | | |
| | | | | | |
	Set Value	October	Case I	Case II	Case III
T-N All nitrogen (inorganic)	Model ((Set Value) - (Environmental standard value) - N dropping speed	39 days	25 days	28 days	18 days
T-P all Phosphorus (inorganic)	((Set Value) - (Environmental standard value) - P dropping speed	9 days	6 days	7 days	4 days
Set Value (Contaminated water):	T - N	0.2 ppm			
	T - P	0.024 ppm			
Environmental Standards:	T - N	0.1 ppm or less			
	T - P	0.015 ppm or less			

Notes

1. The optical condenser is covered by an acrylic sphere, which protects its lens from waves and salty wind. The sphere is cleaned with a special device; a certain chromatic aberration is inevitable due to a single Fresnel Lens. This fact was incorporated in the structural design to primarily allow the visible rays to enter the optical fiber. Thus the condensed value-added solar rays are more useful for producing plants and maintaining their health. The optical energy collected by the optical fiber is carried below the euphotic layer to the lower stratum and used efficiently in

photosynthesis, which is carried out in the optical culture tanks via optical radiators. The test described in this report was conducted in the Nagasaki Prefectural Culture Laboratory at Nobosaki.

References

Mori, K., N. Tanatsuga, and M. Yamashita, "A Visible Solar Ray Supply System for the Space Station," *Acta Astronautica* (*Journal of International Academy of Astronautics*) (Paris, 1985).

Mori, K., "Photoautotrophic Bioreactor Using Visible Solar Rays Condensed by Fresnel Lenses and Transmitted through Optical Fibers," *Biotechnology and Bioengineering Symposium, No. 15* (1985).

Report on Marine Environmental Conservation Surveys Using an Automatic Solar Ray Condensation and Transfer System, commissioned by the Nagasaki Prefectural Government, La Foret Engineering, 1984.

Report on Marine Environmental Conservation Survey, (1985).

The Sunflower: A Basic Study on the Marine Ranch, Sumitomo Heavy Industries and Kajima Construction, January 1986.

Part *IV*

Development of
Human Resources

Chapter 12

Accessibility, Population, and Human Resources

Resio Moses

I am told that in economics the value of a resource is associated with the abundance of that resource. This could also be said of world population. The more people, the less the person's value. Today, more people populate the world than ever before. And I feel that this abundance is one reason why the value of the individual has diminished in relationship to the civilization.

Here in the Pacific, we face a dilemma. If we join the world community, we will become a part of the mass, and our people's importance will diminish when compared to the whole. However, if we remain isolated, we will be able to preserve our individual identity but will lose the technological benefits offered by the world community.

We cannot have it both ways, although I believe that all of us would like to. We must make a choice, and from the choice we make, the direction of our development will follow.

It is my belief that if we, the people of my nation, want to participate meaningfully in the Pacific and world communities, we will have to reorganize our views of life and gear them more to the world view. With our new generation close behind, we will have to decide now whether we should emphasize a reserved existence, or by policy, example, and direction try to establish the Pacific peoples as a real part of the world community. Once this decision is made, I believe we will also find that the methods used to develop our human resources will change.

I am an island boy, and as such I do not feel I can speak about the world as a whole. However, I feel I am qualified to speak about my island nation. I am uncertain that my reflections on the Micronesian experience will touch on concerns that are valid for the rest of the Pacific community. But I hope that some commonality in the issues exists and that in discussions we can broaden the Micronesian-Pacific example to relate to the world community.

Two issues have developed in combination that have changed the direction of human development in the Pacific. One is accessibility to information combined with what I will call "world weight," or the sheer numbers of people inhabiting the earth today. Let me explain what I mean by these two terms.

What is accessibility? It's having information from around the world available to all citizens of the world within a moment's notice. Almost all people today know of space travel, wars, world politics, world diets and drinks, sports, dress, homes, transport, and so on. Just a few short years ago, these same people had not seen the cities of the world or the human drama conveyed to them now through radio, video, TV, movies, telephones, computers, and travel.

Thirty years from now, with the continued expansion of communication-transportation technology, it is possible that every person will be linked as much to the world view as he is to his own traditions, origin, and community environment. Already many of our children know more about space wars, kung-fu, and modern music than they do about fishing, sailing, and a traditional way of life on a tropical island.

What do I mean by world weight? Soon, more than three billion people will live in the world. Over 100,000 of them populate our Micronesian Federation, the FSM, and only about 30,000 live on my own island. This means that if we move into the world community, we must maintain our identity in a sea of humanity where we are outnumbered in greater proportions: that's the weight of the world.

I believe there are several areas in which the impact of these catalysts--accessibility and world weight--will demand a more careful consideration of human resource development in Pacific island nations.

The collapse of transition

We have met transition, and it is U.S. On my island I am transition, and I am growing old. My father was traditional with a love for and a deep knowledge of a now historic culture that is my inheritance. My son will inherit a world view and will hopefully function well in a highly technical, ever broadening global social system. I am the in-between.

The slow transition of traditional societies to the "modern world" has accelerated with the traditional societies collapsing around us. My son, and his generation, must be educated and trained just as are the youth in the most "modern" of nations if he is to interact, compete, and make a contribution to the world being created.

If we are, in reality, completing the transition with my generation, we must carefully consider the goals and objectives of our special training programs, our institutions of higher learning, and our basic educational systems. Our target must be full integration into the technical disciplines, the intricate skilled professions, and the schools of the arts. When we establish institutions of learning, special training courses, and basic educational programs we must not target these systems to produce intermediaries; not almost doctors, or "field engineers," or applied economists, or paralegals, but the real and the true and the bonified highest trained individual the world systems can produce.

Our vanishing richness

With the collapse of transition, the historically accumulated knowledge of our island peoples is being destroyed. My culture is an oral one; no writings, no records, no videos have been recorded. All has been verbally passed from generation to generation, either in people's minds, or personally shown by father to son or by mother to daughter. When our minds are bent in time-consuming schools to better use the tools of the modern world, we lose much of the mind-space and family learning time necessary to carry forward our natural heritage of knowledge and wisdom.

The development of our human resources must include the processes of immediately recording, with all the magnificent tools of the modern world, the oral heritage of magic, myth, music, medicine, understanding of the ocean environment, navigation, custom, belief, social structure, and activity patterns of past Pacific generations so that future generations can, at a more leisurely pace, introduce our unique and specialized knowledge to the world.

It is true that not every citizen can be involved in rigorous formal education. Most of our citizens will rapidly find a working-living niche for themselves too soon after becoming adult. What legacy of human development can we leave these workers? I believe that the best we can do is to provide a very sound primary education for the majority of our people. The majority of our citizens must be able to read and understand, write and communicate, use numbers as a tool in daily living, and speak a world language.

Although this is easy to say, it is not easy to accomplish. Primary school teachers on my own island receive low wages and relatively low professional and community esteem. Thus primary school teachers' physical attendance and as a result their attendance to responsibility and class-room preparation is less than optimal. Classrooms are often not well maintained. School materials and teaching aids are often not available or are not in satisfactory condition. Public interest and expectation of excellence in the basic learning that goes on in the primary schools is absent. But I know as an educator that the very first years of school set the pattern that learning will follow all the years of our lives. We need to look carefully at ourselves in this regard. We need to place more of our resources, more of our expectations, and more appreciation toward our primary educational systems.

The need for emphasizing non-formal, community education-information systems

If the majority of our population has a good, basic education, we must increase the amount of information accessible to our people. We need to provide better content for the on-rushing importation of news, information, styles, products and ideas that our people will receive from the rest of the world. Our mediums of information relay must be improved radio/TV transmission capabilities and programming, interpretive news and educational programs, private newspapers or community newsheets, public meetings and publicly sponsored forums, theater, libraries, and so on. We must consider formal education, for the most part, to become and remain the beginning, not the end, of our human development programs.

The need for reexamining international technical assistance programs and consultancies

For some time now I have felt that many of the technical assistance programs offered to Pacific people do not adequately respond to today's needs.

For example:

a. Many technical assistance programs and technical consultancies underestimate the level of knowledge, skill, and experience that has been so far accumulated by the people of our islands. A large portion of a particular training program or a great deal of an outside technician's work merely repeats to us what we already know.
   Outside technical assistance and short-term teachers must have better knowledge of the capability and experience of the target group here in the islands. Prepackaged programs based on textbook knowledge of the Pacific, or on hearsay, too often do not accomplish what we want them to.
b. Much of our present human resource training is too general to provide workers with the tools needed to adequately tackle everyday operational problems in the public or private sector. We need technical assistance and training that focus on specific, outstanding problems or tasks, not a continual education in general working systems.
c. Many consultancies and experts teach us tools of their trade that are not applicable to our area. National accounting systems and macroeconomic forecasting, demographic modeling, and quantitative analysis in social science and statistics have for the most part limited application for our area. We need a new assessment of the "modern"

world's analytic tools available to us in all disciplines. We need the creation of new and better methods of analyzing small-scale social and economic systems, and we need to learn how to measure the impact that the human factor has on the development problems we face.

d. Many technical training projects and consultancies are too short. I believe it takes us about two years to educate and train an outside expert to know enough about the particular social, economic, and political systems of our state to be of real help in solving development problems. Some of our experts stay only two weeks or three days. More and more we need human resource assistance from people who will stay a long time with particular human development programs, people who will stay through the doing as well as the teaching of how to do.

But just the opposite appears to be happening. It seems international assistance in the Pacific is becoming more regionally oriented, and shorter and shorter projects are scheduled to be spread over the many islands within the region. I hope the time soon comes when international agencies will reassess the efficacy of such short-term programs and consultancies and will place more human resources in a limited number of in-country, long-term programs focused on the follow-through necessary to resolve the development problems we face.

The need for more non-technically oriented education and training

Life is not just maximizing productivity. There is more to it than that. Yet we are all trying to improve our islands in terms of increasing the material products available and measuring and maximizing worker productivity. Would it be possible to bring to our islands a flood of human development programs focused on the arts--theater, music, literature, painting, poetry, and dance? Where are our own sculptors, architects, musicians, actors, artists, and writers? Do our schools teach literature, music theory, design, color, harmony? How can we assess the loss of not cultivating our talents with world knowledge of and perspectives on the arts? How can our individual genius contribute to these creative worlds, and what impact on all our activities would an emphasis on the arts give us? We need to cultivate further our understanding and appreciation of the arts of both East and West.

Outside umbrella administrative programs taking over government functions

More and more, I see technical assistance and consultancies substituting total umbrella administrative programs for individual training: health and hospital administration teams; electrical, power, water, and sewage management teams with 35-year contracts; airlines, ships, financial programming, communications, computers, investment teams that we just plug in as if they were isolated, operational modules parachuted onto our islands. We should be alarmed. The easy task of governments contracting for and assigning whole areas of their operations to foreign administrations is detrimental to the development of our own human resources and their respective accountability.

Internally, we must guard against those options that do not place our people, their skills, and their dedication and integrity on the line. The process of improving and strengthening our public service systems and private businesses is not one of transferring the responsibility of management to foreign administrators, but one of gaining experience for our own workers and demanding of them the skill and knowledge necessary to get the specific work accomplished.

Externally, we ask that serious consideration be given by donor countries to reemphasize the type of assistance needed for us to develop our own human resources. When such human development occurs, we can readily participate in the highly technical, changeable world now accessible to us. We ask that you do not emphasize in your aid and assistance the exportation of administrative-technical consultancies that make it impossible for us to gain the experience, to know the difference, and to anticipate the need for the long-term meaningful development of our own citizens.

Chapter 13

Development of Human Resources: A Singaporean View

Lau Teik Soon

There are many countries in the world that have vast natural resources: they have huge land areas, rich mineral deposits, numerous forest products, and considerable water supplies. On the other hand, there are many states with little, if any, such natural assets. For both categories, however, the pertinent question that should be raised is whether all these resources with which nature has endowed these territories have led to economic growth, peace, progress, and prosperity for the majority of their peoples.

Economic growth is vital because it is directly related to the distribution of income and the standard of living of the people. In turn, it is linked to the political stability as well as the security of the state. The higher the economic growth, the greater the prospect of political stability and security and vice versa.

Whether or not the land, minerals, forests, and waters have been exploited and managed efficiently for the benefit of the population depends to a large extent on a major factor, namely, the quality of the labor resource. Have the people been trained, developed, and utilized to the maximum in order to achieve national goals of economic growth, political stability, and state security? Without the proper development of the labor resource, the other natural assets of the country will not be tapped for the fullest benefit of the people.

For the proper and effective management of the latent wealth of the country as well as the organization of the state itself, a labor force must be trained and nurtured to its fullest potential. From this resource comes, first, the personnel for the key leadership roles in society--for example, politics, government, industry, and agriculture; second, the capable and efficient officers for the judicial and administrative services; and third, the skilled and unskilled labor force for the public and private sectors. If the human resource is properly developed to fulfill these various functions, then it will be possible for the country to achieve success in the economic, political, and security fields.

To provide capable, self-reliant, and dedicated leadership in society, there must be developed what may be called a leadership culture. The leadership culture has certain significant features. First, it is founded primarily on meritocracy, that is, merit and reward for those people who deserve them based on objective criteria, mainly educational qualifications, proven ability, and relevant experience. Leaders must be trained and well educated at least up to the tertiary level because they are required to manage efficiently the modern and complex state organization and its institutions in order to achieve the societal goals. They must have the opportunity to gain experience and to prove that they have the ability to provide leadership. Leaders are not made; they emerge after years of education and working experience. They rise rapidly through the ranks and take on decision-making positions in politics, government, administration, and the economy.

Second, the leadership culture should emphasize the morality of the leaders, focusing on such qualities as honesty, integrity, and service. It should focus on the commitment and dedication to serve the people and to achieve the national goals. For example, political leaders should regard their appointments as an opportunity to do something worthwhile for the nation and the people. They should adopt the John F. Kennedy axiom: Ask not what your country can do for you but what you can do for your country. In fact, qualified, well-placed, and successful people would have to make certain personal and material sacrifices to serve in political office.

Last but not least, a leadership culture allows for the self-reliant and decisive action of the leaders who are confronted with the minimum of constraints imposed by the society. For example, if a policy is considered to be beneficial for the majority of people, then every effort would be made to implement it regardless of the obstacles.

In the developing states, it is crucial that the administrative and judicial arms of the state be strong, efficient, and impartial. The best of the labor resource should be channeled to these institutions. For example, the top graduates from the universities should be offered admission into these services. This is necessary because the civil and judicial officers implement the decisions of the government and administer the laws of the land; many of them remain for a lifetime in their chosen careers. More significantly, the political leaders rely on them to provide sound advice and recommendations so that the former can formulate policies designed to serve the interests of the people. So it seems logical that the top brain power should be selected for the key services of the state. Toward this end, scholarships must be provided for the bright young students who, on graduation, will join the administrative and judicial services. In subsequent years, the more efficient ones will be rewarded through promotion and recognition.

In general, the labor resource of a country should be well trained and equipped with knowledge and skills so that the majority of the people can obtain employment and maintain a decent standard of living. In this connection, it is vital to provide sufficient graduates, technicians, and skilled personnel to the job market. Thus there should be a plan to provide for the various types of labor force in the future. For example, based on present and projected needs, the government may decide that they would need a certain number of engineers, computer programmers, electrical technicians, and welders in five to ten years' time. Then the universities, polytechnics, technical schools, and other educational institutions would gear their admission to these projected labor force requirements.

The caliber of the labor force should be of the highest standard. Students and undergraduates should be trained to meet international standards so that they can keep up with the latest knowledge and technology and be competitive in the world market. For example, if they have the required expertise, they could be employed at the local or foreign offices of the multinational companies. Such flexibility of the labor force provides the impetus for the attainment of still higher levels of achievements.

Whatever the level of the human resource, there must be the prospect for upward mobility--for example, for a skilled technician to reach an administrative position. But the promotion must be based on objective criteria, namely, educational qualifications, experience, and proven ability. There must be the opportunity at each level to acquire the necessary academic and technical standards. Employers must encourage and support financially their employees who are prepared to better their qualifications.

To maintain the high standard of the labor force, an open system of rewards and punishment must be institutionalized. Rewards should go to those who have ability and who strive toward the achievement of the national goals; rewards can be in the form of monetary awards, status, and public recognition. As for punishment, it must be clear to everyone from the outset that those who are negligent or corrupt should not go unpunished. For example, there are cases in some countries where leading politicians and civil servants have been given imprisonment, fines, or dismissal for offenses committed. Such punishment must apply to all so that it is generally known in society that no one can be exempted from the penalty. If there exists any form of discrimination, then there will be no incentive for honest people to work hard, especially when they realize that the reward goes to less-than-qualified or -experienced people.

In general, the development of the human resource must be a harmonious one so that there is a minimum of dissent and dissatisfaction in the society. If one's station in life is the result of objective factors, then there will be a minimum of disharmony. For example, a new university graduate and a recent high school graduate, both without experience, would not receive the same payment because they have different training and qualifications; they would be employed at different levels with separate terms and conditions of service. But the incentive must be there for the less qualified to obtain the better qualification. The awareness that there is an open system of recruitment and opportunity for upward mobility through better education and experience would give rise to harmony in the society.

The development and utility of the human resource, as I have described it, may be subject to various limitations owing to the national characteristics of various countries. Such political, cultural, and economic limitations often make it difficult for the state to develop and utilize its labor force in the best way possible. Ultimately, the manner in which the human resource has been managed will be reflected in the rate of economic growth, the level of political stability, and the well-being and security of the country.

Part V

Issues and Directions

Chapter 14

Aid and Development

R. Gordon Jackson

Like everyone else at this forum, I speak in a personal capacity, not on behalf of any organization or country.

My remarks will be mainly about where we go from here. How can we make the twenty-first century better for haumanity, in the Pacific and globally, than this has been? Relative to other parts of the world, the South Pacific is not short of aid, and it seems that more is on the way from new donors, especially Japan.

There are some general principles worth recalling.

Why is aid given at all? In the aid business, not everyone is a suli, or heir, of the global community. Motives cover a broad range from the totally altruistic to the totally self-seeking. For me, the fundamental drive can be seen as reverence for life, or "love thy neighbor," or the idea of kinship, leading to a sense of responsibility for others of the human community. These values are altruistic, but they extend in the direction of self-interest. Doing good works is good not only for one's standing in the eyes of others but also for one's own self-esteem. More important, a world more just and equal is likely to be more stable and peaceful, and better also for trade and investment. Historical ties, geography, political preferences, and strategic interests also influence attitudes to aid. But aid that is heavily tied and aid that is given to buy political support is likely to be resented.

In an ideal world, values and goals would be humanity centered and long-term rather than nation-centered and short-term. Concerned individuals exert themselves to hasten the transformation toward global values. But in any one country, aid policy, to be successful, cannot be too far ahead of the mix of values as they are. Now, nobody has ever referred to Australia, Inc. We don't have a leadership culture. But with the mix of values as they are, there is broad general support in my country for a significant aid program, primarily for humanitarian reasons, to share prosperity through economic and social development. Aid also complements strategic and economic interests, and by helping developing countries to grow, it provides economic opportunities for our own people. Community support for aid depends on all of these mandates. And among recipient countries, we accord the highest priority to Papua New Guinea and the small island nations of the Pacific and Indian oceans.

Sustained development depends on growth with equity. Without growth, there won't be much to redistribute. Without equity, growth doesn't lead to development. So aid policy should focus on helping developing countries achieve growth that alleviates poverty and improves income distribution.

However, on the world scene, aid has made only a marginal contribution to development. As Professor Walt Rostow said, the percentage that comes from outside is very small. The presence or absence of growth, and the rate of it, depends for the most part on domestic institutional arrangements and domestic policies. Growth does not depend particularly on such structural characteristics as a country's natural resources, size, or location. Many resource-rich countries have a poor growth record, whereas some small countries, some land-locked countries, and some that are very distant from world markets have grown rapidly. Nor is growth correlated with the present level of development: the relatively developed countries of Latin America are among the slowest growing. Nor is it the international environment, which is pretty much the same for all.

Nor, it seems, is a long period of political stability a necessary condition for growth. Indeed, it may be that the longer a society enjoys political stability, the more likely it is to develop powerful special-interest lobbies that make it less efficient economically. Conversely, the trauma of revolution or defeat in war may facilitate subsequent growth by sweeping away social rigidities and institutional barriers to change.

What is necessary for development is an attitude of mind that wants that development, a stable economic environment that encourages savings, investment, and the efficient allocation and use of resources, and a social environment that promotes an equitable distribution of the benefits of growth. We can observe that those developing countries that have promoted trade and have pursued outward-looking economic policies have achieved faster growth, fuller employment, and higher wages than those that have clung to protection. And there is a strong correlation between development and the quality of government.

Governor Resio Moses made some very wise observations about management of aid. Three years ago, some colleagues and I urged my government to make a major change in the way we manage aid. We used to build up aid programs largely by responding to shopping lists of the recipient countries, some of which were well thought out, others less so. We made many mistakes. Now we are trying to build up an aid strategy toward each developing country by studying and understanding its development situation, processes, and needs so as to identify some of its critical constraints to development. Some progress has been made, but there is a long way to go. We then try to form a consensus with the recipient country on the design of aid programs targeted at selected critical constraints. I would suggest that this is the process by which aid programs should be developed. For our part, we would prefer to apply the aid to critical constraints on growth.

Australia has been a steadfast financial supporter of the World Bank, the Asian Development Bank, and the various United Nations agencies concerned with development. However, each of them is a large bureaucracy with very substantial internal costs. We are looking more and more critically at the performance of each, asking what value does it add to our taxpayers' dollar in terms of aid or service delivered to the developing country?

Those are some general principles. Turning now to the South Pacific, the problem is that critical constraints to growth abound, some of which may yield to aid wisely designed and effectively delivered, and some of which will not. Three sorts of constraints are obvious:

- natural constraints (of geography and resources);
- constraints that are inherited or acquired; and
- those that arise form the pressures of rapid change, both domestic and external.

Less obvious and more subtle is another constraint, something of a paradox. For the smaller island nations, elements of the aid process itself may actually inhibit growth! As we were told in this forum, aid donors may not have all the answers, and what answers they do have may sometimes only mess things up.

If we look at the growth record in the South Pacific, it is not too successful. The data are rather sketchy, but I have seen calculations by the Australian Development Assistance Bureau that seem to indicate that over a period from approximately 1976 to 1985 only in Tonga and Cook Islands did GNP per capita increase, and that only slightly. Over that period, GNP per capita in Fiji, the Solomons, Vanuatu, Western Samoa, Kiribati, and Tuvalu actually fell. If aid is to promote growth, we haven't been doing it right.

Aid brings negatives as well as positives. As has been said here, it can be corrosive. In the words of Peter Drysdale, aid can corrupt economic management. In this part of the world, aid works to enlarge the public sector and to keep down the private sector. It tends to draw resources away form the production of goods. It tends to keep exchange rates strong, to the competitive disadvantage of island industries that produce for export. More aid makes more demands on the limited resources of a receiving government to manage it.

The relative magnitudes are such that a multilateral agency or a single bilateral donor can exercise a large degree of dominance, whether intended or not. So as we increase aid flows to the small island nations, we must try correspondingly harder to be more sensitive, to put the recipient point of view ahead of the donor point of view.

We must try not to overrun the islands, in Charles Lepani's phrase, with agencies and donors. We need some better coordination to improve the balance between

- countries in terms of aid;
- public and private sectors;
- infrastructure and the production of goods for consumption and trade; and
- showpiece construction jobs and recurrent funding.

We need to leave a place--I would hope an increasingly important place--for delivery of part of the aid through church and other voluntary agencies. We need coordination, but we should be cautious about imposing it from outside. Perhaps the South Pacific countries themselves might consider setting up an aid coordination mechanism for the region.

So much for aid. But world-wide, trade flows are far more important than aid flows. In the long run, the justice and dignity of the peoples of the South Pacific will be better served by trade. But as Rasheed Ali so eloquently said, markets for tropical farm commodities are devastated by subsidy practices of the industrialized countries. As another participant pointed out, technology and aid won't benefit the Pacific much if great barriers remain on the access to markets.

The Pacific idea is a powerful idea of great attraction. But there is more in the Pacific than the rim. To nurture the Pacific idea, we need rules of the game that are no more and no less than are needed to relax global tensions in these troubled and restless times.

It seems to me that most countries need more rather than fewer facilities to make painful economic adjustments. If a country can't or won't exercise fiscal balance, there has to be an adjustment somewhere, and these days it often falls on the exchange rate. So, as floating exchange rates help adjustment, we ought to keep them floating. But we need great changes in the rules of the trade game. As global citizens, we should each do what we can in our own constituencies to promote a healthier trade regime. We should work in our own different ways toward future rules of the trade game that are multilateral rather than bilateral. There should be rules of the game for agriculture as well as for manufactures, and for tropical agriculture as well as for temperate agriculture; there should be less protection in the industrialized countries and fewer subsidies. There should be a little more sensitivity to the particular trade needs and concerns of the small island nations of the South Pacific.

Chapter 15

A Commonwealth of Free and Prospering Nations

Mohammad Sadli

First of all, please allow me to express my sincere appreciation for the chance to take part in a small way in this international conference from so far away as Kuala Lumpur.

At the moment I am taking part in a conference on ASEAN economic cooperation. In our region, there have been many such conferences lately because at the end of the year there will be a summit meeting of the heads of states and governments of the ASEAN member countries. The last conference was ten years ago. Since then, the principles of economic cooperation, basically a system of giving each other trade preferences and not a common market of free trade regime as in Europe, have not been executed forcefully. Economic nationalism and protectionist sentiments have had the upper hand.

ASEAN is another example of the difficulties that arise when developing countries want to get together and integrate their economies. You either get a "no results" situation as in ASEAN, or an equally frustrating experience of trade frictions, such as that of Latin America. But the spirit of wanting to relate to each other politically, socially, and economically remains strong, and that is what ASEAN is all about.

ASEAN countries are open economies with high economic growth rates in the past. Such economic growth has been the product of an outward looking and global trade orientation. That is why skeptics are asking to what extent a regional market integration among developing countries could contribute significantly to the economic growth of the participating countries. Such regional economic cooperation can never be a good substitute for world-wide trade cooperation. That is why ASEAN will remain an outward-looking economic grouping, fully endorsing and participating in the GATT new round. But we remain a strong believer in regional cooperation and not only for its immediate economic benefits.

That is why we from ASEAN welcome the idea of weaving stronger ties with other Pacific developing countries, although many thousand miles of water separate us from each another. Our motive is partly idealistic, because we do not know what we can do for each other directly. The idea of South-South cooperation and technical cooperation among developing countries attracts us. But we are aware that implementation is fraught with difficulties, especially with respect to government projects. Technical cooperation between ASEAN governments is also not a big affair and is often made possible only by grants from donor countries.

Perhaps we should get to know each other better and build a sense of community before we start doing practical things. It was the same in ASEAN. We spent the first ten, perhaps twenty years, forging a feeling of familiarity among nations that had long been separated by their colonial histories. Although our diplomats, our government officials, and our business executives can call each other now by telephone, few business transactions have yet been forthcoming.

Our links for progress have first of all been with the richer industrialized countries. Japan, the United States, and Europe are our major trading partners, and that will remain so. The middle-sized industrial countries, such as Australia, Canada, and New Zealand, are also regular dialogue partners for ASEAN. More recently, with the strong economic growth of the newly industrializing countries, such as South Korea, Taiwan, and Hong Kong, our trade with them is expanding fast because of emerging complementarities. Even trade with a lesser-developed country, for example, the PRC, is blossoming because of its own complementarities. Singapore, for instance, exports technical services to assist the Chinese hotels, and even Indonesia manages to have an export surplus.

We look forward to seeing a wider Pacific community with the South Pacific countries participating fully. The purpose is not only more trade and more internal advancement. If we have more understanding, more appreciation for each other, and more willingness to share, it will make all of us richer, not only in a material sense but perhaps, more important, in a spiritual sense. We would like to live in a commonwealth of free and prospering nations in a true ocean of peace.

Chapter 16

The United States and the Asia-Pacific Region

John D. Rockefeller IV

My family has had a deep reverence for the Asian peoples and their cultures for decades. The three years I spent as a young man in Japan were among the most satisfying and stimulating in my life. That was the beginning of a lifelong interest in Asia.

At the start of this century, U.S. Secretary of State John Hay spoke at the ceremony to open the Panama Canal: "The Mediterranean," he said, "is the ocean of the past; the Atlantic the ocean of the present and the Pacific the ocean of the future." Today, nearly 90 years later, we can appreciate his remarkable prescience. The future has indeed arrived.

In economic development, in the emergence of democratic political institutions, and in global influence, the Asia-Pacific region has established itself as a world leader. "Pacific awareness" is gaining momentum in the United States--not only on our West Coast but in many areas, and particularly in our nation's capital. Economically, as well as politically, strategically, and demographically, the Pacific region is crucial to the United States' present and to United States' future. And our future will be equally crucial for the Pacific. Interdependence is not simply a cliche. It is a fact of life.

The destinies of the developing nations in East Asia and the Pacific rely on healthy market interaction and long-term domestic and regional stability. Economic prosperity and political stability are fundamentally intertwined and interdependent--the decline of one unavoidably leads to the weakening of another.

Looking at the likely development of the Asia-Pacific region over the coming decades, it is evident that the stakes are high and the prospects exciting. All of you are quite familiar with the phenomenal economic success of the Pacific region during the past 15 years. The newly industrializing countries (NICS) of Asia plus the six members of ASEAN have outperformed all other developing nations in real growth per capita, growth of exports, control of inflation, and expansion of savings and investment. With few available natural resources, governments in Singapore, Taiwan, South Korea, and Japan, among others, bet on human resources as the key to economic success. Through education and training, they have made truly impressive progress.

U.S. trade with the Pacific rim region surpassed that with the Atlantic as early as 1975, and the gap continues to grow every year. In 1981, the United States' trade with East Asia was $15 billion larger than its trade with Europe. By 1986, the difference had grown to $61 billion. And the flow of trade is not one way. Although we are experiencing some serious bilateral trade deficits at present, the Pacific continues to be a strong market for U.S. goods. Japan, Korea, Australia, and Taiwan are among the United States' 10 largest customers, and we sell more to ASEAN nations than we do to all of South America.

The countries of Asia and the Pacific have, historically, been divided by differences in ethnic, religious, and cultural values. Suspicious of each other and harboring long memories of exploitation, they have been slow to build cooperative institutions. But the region is becoming increasingly interdependent. With the exception of the United States and Canada, each nation in the region conducts more than half its trade with other countries in the region.

Right now, the main source of tension between the Pacific area and the rest of the extended Western alliance is economic-protectionist temptations in Europe and the United States on the one hand, and the protection of domestic markets throughout much of the Asia-Pacific region on the other.

If the United States is able to gain control of its trade and budget deficits, if Japan makes its market more accessible to imports, if Korea and Taiwan keep on their current path toward trade and investment liberalization, and if all markets strive to keep their markets open, the region will continue to realize a high growth rate. Conversely, if the U.S. response to the trade challenge is protectionism, if Japan's market remains import-resistant, and if restricted financial markets, closed import regimes, and managed export policies prevail, economic vitality in the region will undoubtedly decline.

It is a time for adjustment--economic adjustment as well as political. The reasons are obvious. In order to sustain and improve conditions necessary for high levels of growth and prosperity, we must strive to open up markets and ward off protectionism. And in order to promote political stability, we must support the further growth of democracy and freedom among the diverse and unique societies of the region.

The trend of several emerging democracies in the region toward political stability is quite encouraging, even exciting. In the Philippines we have witnessed the strength of "people power," the revitalization of democracy, and significant constitutional reform. In Korea, where steps have been taken toward popular participation in a truly representative government, there is great hope for future stability. In Taiwan, martial law has ended after four decades, and the opposition, although small, has been granted legal status. We are pleased to see democratic processes taking root and are confident they will facilitate stability and prosperity throughout the entire region.

The United States is serious in its commitment to assist the independent, democratic island nations of the South Pacific.

After lengthy negotiations, a regional fisheries treaty between the United States and the 16-member nations of the Forum Fisheries Agency was concluded. Since our differences with the region over this issue have been exploited by our adversaries, the treaty addresses national security concerns as well as our economic relationships in the area. The treaty is intended to resolve a serious dispute between the United States and the nations of the region, and also to assist in the development of an indigenous fishing industry and more vigorous local economies.

We have witnessed great progress in the region toward political and social development in countries that share our democratic values and commitment to human rights. Since the enactment of the compact legislation for freely associated states in 1986, the Marshall Islands and the Federated States of Micronesia have made a remarkably smooth transition to independence. There is great hope that Palau will follow suit by meeting its constitutional requirements for approval of the Compact of Free Association.

While the United States maintains a formal commitment to regional security in the Asia-Pacific region, we by no means seek a position of dominance there. We do, however, seek to ensure that no other state or combination of states achieves such dominance. Our military relationships are based on mutual benefits: the U.S. Japanese Security Treaty, the integrated United Nation Command in Korea, our security agreement with Thailand, and our base agreements with the Philippines are all manifestations of the same spirit. Although we are presently going through serious problems with New Zealand, our ANZUS relationship with Australia is unshakable. We are confident that the fundamental strength of our relations with the South Pacific region will lead to a resolution of the issues that separate us.

Along those lines, I must mention that the most notable, and unfortunate, recent development in the Pacific region has been increased attention from the Soviet Union. General Secretary Gorbachev's Vladivostok address of July 1986 suggested that Moscow's Asia policy has assumed a position of increased importance over the past few years. Gorbachev spoke of nurturing political and economic ties with the small island states of the South Pacific, of supporting New Zealand's antinuclear policies, and of promoting the cause of a South Pacific nuclear-free zone. He suggested to the new Philippine government that an end to U.S. access to military bases there would not go "unanswered," and he proposed various so-called "confidence-building" measures.

In late November 1985, the Soviet Union added the first nuclear-powered cruiser to its forces in Asia. From a defensive fleet of 200 warships in 1960, the Soviet force has grown to more than 800 vessels world-wide with virtually all the capabilities of a modern "blue-water" navy. And the Soviet Union's Pacific Fleet is now its largest. In an area that has been remarkably free of great power rivalry, we are watching closely to see whether this new Soviet power will translate into efforts at destabilization.

East Asia and the Pacific is a tremendously fertile and dynamic region. It possesses great potential, not only for its own development but also for the promotion of global prosperity and security as a whole. Our goals and the goals of the entire Asia-Pacific community have become increasingly interdependent. The United States is as much a Pacific nation as it is an Atlantic nation, and we are determined to work together--to consult, to combine our resources efficiently, and to form a strong regional partnership. Together we must rise to the challenges ahead.

Ambassador Mike Mansfield has said many times that the United States' future is in Asia. I think we can all agree with him. The American people must prepare to take advantage of the mounting opportunities to forge a healthy partnership with the Asia-Pacific region. We must shape policies with an eye to the future--by learning Asian languages and history, and by identifying common interests, challenges, and responsibilities. Only through frequent consultation can we facilitate mutual understanding and secure enduring peace and prosperity.

Appendixes

Appendix A

Preliminary Survey on Young Pacific Islanders' Value Concept

Introduction

In recent years, as the ratio of Japan's economy in the world economy has increased, its international responsibility has increased both quantitatively and qualitatively. As a result, Japan's Official Development Assistance (ODA) has been showing a steady growth. Nevertheless, domestically, not enough understanding and support has yet been acquired under a difficult administrative and financial situation, and externally, all the more promotion of development cooperation according to the national power is required both from the DAC member countries and developing countries.

As the background to such needs and requirements, it could be said that the ODA of Japan has been rather concentrated to a specific area and/or country, and that priority has been put on types of economic development, causing lack of mobility and efficiency.

Therefore, all the more needed in the future is more effective and efficient implementation of development cooperation. Attitudes for promoting and widening the field of cooperation regardless of the size of the recipient countries, the scale of the economic relationships, and the distance of the area are necessary.

With these circumstances in mind, there is consideration of the "Pacific Age," and many discussions are being carried on concerning the ways of

This appendix, prepared by the Association for Promotion of International Cooperation, is an outcome of a research project funded and supported by the Japan Shipbuilding Industry Foundation.

thinking on this issue. There are many small but various and vital "young" countries lying sporadically over the Pacific area, that have potentialities in no way inferior to those of other Pacific-rim areas, such as Southeast Asia and Central and South America. However, relationships between Japan and this area are not yet considered sufficiently evolved and are left for future development.

Since these small island countries in the Pacific do not have much population or land-area, and since their history is rather "young," they have just begun the course of their development. The expectation for Japan, which has become an economic power and one of the largest cooperation donors in the free world, is highly counted on. Nevertheless, since the island countries are very cautious about the evil effects of past development activities that could easily destroy the small-scale economy, society, and culture, and since they have a great deal of pride and self-respect in their own traditions and cultures, a careful approach is taken in cooperating with Japan.

On the other hand, to promote a wider range of international cooperation and exchange and to implement development cooperation that is more effective, efficient, and suitable for the needs of the recipient countries, Japan must carefully think through the expansion of cooperation measures. It is essential for Japan to seek out the most acceptable form of cooperation, one that would originate with the needs and values of the recipient people and the

Accordingly, in this survey, we have focused on the young people in the Pacific area who will actively participate in the course of development of their countries and/or the area in the near future. We have drawn up a questionnaire concerning their thinking, hopes, and consciousness about the general idea of development, interests, and evaluation of development activities with bilateral countries and international agencies, and the need of cooperation with Japan to make known their way of thinking and to consider together the ideal way of cooperation in the future.

Results of the questionnaire

a. Profile of the respondents

In this questionnaire survey, there were 413 respondents from the following seven countries and one area.

Fiji	151
Niue	28
Papua New Guinea	105
Solomon Islands	68
Vanuatu	21
Western Samoa	26
Tonga	2
Cook Islands	12

A general profile of these respondents is as follows:

1. Of the total 413, 269 are male and 124 are female (excluding the "no answers," of which there are 20), thus making the ratio of the sexes about 2 to 1.
2. Concerning age, around 70 percent are in their late teens and early twenties. The average age of the respondents is calculated to be 20.9 years.
3. Concerning marital status, more than 80 percent are single.
4. Professionally, more than 60 percent are "students" (61.2 percent), followed by "public servants" (16.3 percent) and "farmers" (including fishermen, woodsmen, and ranchmen) (8.4 percent). There are very few "employees" of private enterprises (6.0 percent).

b. Consciousness of "development"

Consciousness of the word development is very high, as expected: 98.9 percent of males and 95.9 percent of females responded positively.

Of these, 87.6 percent think of "development" as "favorable," and 7.8 percent think of it as "unfavorable" (the remaining 4.6 percent were "no answer"). The main reason for thinking of "development" as "favorable" is that "It promotes opportunities for people."

As this option is considered in somewhat metaphysical terms, its choice well reflects the high priority placed on respecting the unique cultures and values of the Pacific area. Much attention should be paid to the fact that this option was chosen over the other option of "It makes the country economically rich."

On the other hand, as reasons for thinking of "development" as "unfavorable," all the options such as "It destroys the traditional values and thinking," "It destroys the environment," "It corrupts social stability" and/or "It brings a monetary economy to a self-sufficient community and invites mammonism," were given generally high scores. From these results, it can be said that the evil effects attendant upon the course of development are well anticipated and recognized.

Another finding is that the pace of development "must take place with well-balanced timing and should not disturb the traditional culture and values or the natural environment." As this opinion is most understandable, it should be noted that the option of "Development should take place as slowly as possible." was chosen three times as often as the option of "Development must take place as rapidly as possible." This opinion also reveals the way of thinking in the Pacific area.

c.   Recognition of "development cooperation"

In the recognition of "development cooperation" by bilateral countries and multilateral organizations, 86 percent think positively that such cooperations have been taking an active role in development , 10 times more than those who have a negative opinion (8.3 percent). The main reason for the negative attitude toward "development cooperation" was interference by foreign countries.

In answer to the question "In which field do you think this is true?" "economically" and "educationally" got higher scores, but "environmentally" and "culturally" got rather low recognition. From this observation, it could be said that, should cooperation in the future focus attention on the latter fields, then it will meet the needs in the Pacific area.

As to type of "development cooperation," bilateral cooperation is more recognized than multilateral cooperation, and intraregional cooperation gets only 5 percent recognition. However, as is mentioned below, there is not much preference between bilateral cooperation and multilateral cooperation in expecting an ideal type of cooperation. But there appear to be considerable differences depending on each country's historical and geopolitical situations, suggesting the need for carefully thought out measures for conducting "development cooperation."

As bilateral donors, Australia, Japan, New Zealand, the United Kingdom, and the United States received much recognition and evaluation. Other than the DAC member countries, it is noted that the People's Republic of China unexpectedly received a rather high score. France, which is supposed to have much prestige in the Pacific area, received far less recognition than China and less than West Germany. As multilateral donors, male respondents gave much attention to funding agencies such as the World Bank and the Asian Development Bank, whereas female respondents counted highly such agencies as WHO, UNESCO, and UNICEF, all of which are conducting activities closely related to daily life.

d.   Perspectives on "intraregional cooperation" and the "development of the Pacific area"

Youth in the Pacific area show much concern for and interest in intraregional organizations such as the SPC, SPF, and SPEC. Even the respondents who did not know of such organizations showed interest in finding out all about them.

The activities and effects of such intraregional organizations were highly evaluated, and the option of "It is doubtful if such intraregional cooperation can attain fruitful results" is given only a low score. However, as those organizations lack positive achievement of projects and/or programs, another option of "It is essential for other countries and/or international organizations to participate in such intraregional organizations" gets 20 percent backing.

From the perspective of intraregional cooperation, nearly 70 percent of respondents answered positively to the option that "Pacific basin cooperation will be further promoted for the overall development of the area," while the cautious statement that "Pacific basin cooperation will continue at the present level" scored only 26 percent. It can be concluded that, although the youth in the Pacific area highly rated the intraregional organizations highly, they were not overestimating their real capabilities.

From the perspective of "development of the Pacific area," nearly 60 percent of respondents thought that "The Pacific basin will develop but not like other countries or areas (for example: with its own values and cultures)," greatly exceeding the number who thought that "The Pacific basin will develop like other developed countries and areas (for example, will become economically rich, and so on)." This is further evidence of the Pacific way of thinking.

e. Opinion on "development cooperation from Japan"

There were high expectations (94.8 percent) concerning "development cooperation from Japan."

"Technical cooperation" was counted high, while "human-resources development" and "cultural and academic interchanges" were not evaluated as anticipated. These findings may have resulted from their recognition of Japan mainly as an economic and technical power, and from a lack of mutual understanding between them and Japan.

As for the reasons for the negative answer on "development cooperation from Japan," most of them were "We receive enough cooperation from other sources" and "We can manage by ourselves," reflecting not so much anti-Japanese sentiment as a lack of the presence of Japan in this area.

f. Recognition of the "role of youth" and "international exchange"

As for the role of youth in development, more than 75 percent of respondents thought that "Youth should actively participate in the development of their own country and/or the area." Including the 20 percent that expressed agreement with the statement that "Youth should study hard to prepare for the futuret ake-over by national and regional leaderships," a great number showed interest in actively participating in the course of development. Only two respondents thought that "Youth should pursue their own pleasure and not worry about development."

The majority also expressed a positive attitude toward "international exchange." Excluding the "no answer," 94.8 percent of respondents answered had a positive opinion on both visiting foreign countries and receiving foreign guests. There were seven respondents who answered negatively to both the latter. All of them were Solomon Islanders reflecting the unique nature of their country.

Concluding remarks and proposals

The results of the survey generally confirmed expectations held before the implementation of the survey. However, in looking into the details by sex, age-group, country, and profession, many differences and unexpected opinions were observed.

A general summary of the survey is as follows:

a. Consciousness of development is very high and the zeal for it is strong.
b. As for the course of development, it is to be directed to a slow and not economically biased one, keeping the countries' own unique cultures and values in mind.
c. Cooperations on development from outside donors is much praised and recognized, although respondents feel such cooperation is rather focused on economic and educational fields. Ratings on cultural and environmental cooperation, on which respondents put high importance for their course of development, are not yet high.
d. Respondents do not care whether the donors of development cooperation are bilateral countries or multilateral agencies.
e. Concerning intraregional cooperation, although the evaluation of existing intraregional organizations is not high, these organizations are expected to become more active and practical.
f. In general, it is believed that the Pacific area will develop in the future with their unique culture and tradition, but not like other areas where the purpose of development is mainly economic.
g. Many expectations are held for development cooperation from Japan. However, economic and technical cooperation is emphasized, while cultural and academic is not
h. The great majority responded positively to participating in the course of national and/or regional development as a role for youth.
i. A great majority also supported the promotion of international exchanges, excluding negative opinions on a specific country.
j. Several differences were observed among the sexes, countries, age-groups, and professions of the respondents. It should be kept in mind that the opinion of the total area may be slightly different

from that of specific sex, age, professional and especially national groups of the respondents.

Based on the above summary, proposals are made concerning international cooperation between Japan and the Pacific area to promote and strengthen mutual relationships.

The first half of the proposals relate to the general relationship between Japan and the Pacific area by examining the way of thinking, attitudes, and procedures in cooperating with each other.

In the latter part, especially concerning the relationship with young people in the Pacific area, concrete means for cooperation are considered and proposed including the setting up of the South Pacific Youth Forum, which would activate existing organizations and promote new intraregional and international exchanges.

Appendix B

To Promote Economic Self-Reliance: A Proposal for Pacific Island Countries

Historical overview of Pacific island vulnerabilities

> Political stability and constitutionalism have been features of the post colonial area in Oceania. . . .There has, indeed, been no coup; and there has been no change of government in Oceania that has not been constitutional.[1]

The above comment of Barrie MacDonald is shared on the whole by all specialists on the Pacific islands region.

This long-standing perception of the Pacific islands, however, has been crushed abruptly by a military coup d'etat that took place in Fiji in May 1987. Some observers may have forecast the defeat of the Alliance party in the election held in April, but nobody predicted a military coup. We now must ponder the relationships between the internal and external factors peculiar to Fiji, and the factors of potential insecurity hidden beneath the socioeconomic developments of the Pacific island countries in general.

First, we should like to look back at the sociopolitical changes that have taken place in the Pacific islands region during the last two decades so as to clarify the merits and demerits of external aid and aid-dependent development programs.

This appendix was prepared by Terutaro Nishino, Sophia University.

From the beginning of the 1970s, a new "Pacific Way" movement has been advocated by the Fijian Prime Minister. This has helped generate a genuine and progressive attempt by young intellectuals to forge a new regional identity for themselves. The Pacific Way became very popular with the new political leaders, so much so that they even sponsored, in due time, a Pacific Islands Conference to discuss "Development the Pacific Way."

On the other hand, the Pacific island countries became increasingly concerned over the serious constraints placed on their developmental aspirations caused by the unequal geographic size and the varied natural and human resources among them. Two noteworthy trends emerged from this situation.

The first was the "Melanesian Way," launched by Papua New Guinean leaders to reflect an egalitarian movement. The indigenous customary societies in Melanesian countries are not similar to the Polynesian traditional societies. And the Melanesian leaders took the Pacific Way as a movement biased towards Polynesian ideas.

The second was a regional consensus to classify the island countries according to geographic size and resources. The classification has been realized in the provisions of the South Pacific Regional Trade and Economic Cooperation Agreement (SPARTECA). This agreement classified the Forum Island Countries (FICs) into two groups, namely by distinguishing the smaller FICs from other FICs.

Since 1980, the year when the Anglo-French Condominium of New Hebrides attained independence as the Republic of Vanuatu, the Pacific island countries have been involved in varying degrees of political turmoil around them.

> If there were such a thing as a political strongwind signal, it would have been hoisted in the South Pacific in 1981 as a warning of troubled times ahead. In the year of 1980, the Kanak independence struggle in New Caledonia, the protest movement against nuclear testing and nuclear wastes dumping in the Pacific, and the critical opinions against illegal tuna fishing in the Pacific island countries' EEZ have been intensified simultaneously. After the tranquil years of the 1960-1970s when the states moved to independence in what was an ocean of political calm, the coming decade promises to be one of radicalization.[2]

From the Pacific islanders' point of view, the Pacific has been rapidly becoming an area of intense competition, conflict ,and struggle. We would like to quote the following from a statement adopted at the Fourth Assembly of the Pacific Conference of Churches (PCC) convened at Nukualofa in May 1981.

It is becoming clear that even though many Pacific nations have their political independence, new kinds of colonialism are taking over, and with great force. So we are concerned about the profound human rights implications in the attitude that the Pacific Ocean, its islands and its peoples may be sued for narrow and selfish purposes by whoever have the brazen power to do so. At this moment we see this power wielded more in the economic sense than in military terms and exercised in ways more subtle than direct.

The above statement alluded to the Pacific Basin Cooperation Concept (PBCC) as promoted by Japan. It appeared after accusations had been made that France had made nuclear tests and after the United States and Japan had made a nuclear wastes dumping proposal, amid indecisive attitudes toward decolonization. The islanders regarded the PBCC as a strategy representing an unfortunate reinforcement of existing relationships of power and control in the Pacific. We must, however, say that their perception of the PBCC was perhaps based on misconceptions.

Well-informed writers assumed, at the beginning of the 1980s, that regional security issues were focused on nuclear matters, decolonization, and fishing. And they thought that the principal military question would be neither nuclear nor decolonization but fishing. They were worrying about the means of conducting surveillance of the EEZ that could inevitably have strategic implications.

Today, as we approach the end of the 1980s, the above-noted three security issues are entering into a new phase. During the past few years, the three issues have become intermingled. The accelerated Kanak independence struggles in New Caledonia continue to have the most striking impact on the South Pacific region. The diplomatic stance of Vanuatu has been motivated by her hostility toward French colonialist policies in New Caledonia, and this may have inspired Libyan activities in the South Pacific recently.

The changed American attitude toward tuna fishing in the Pacific has helped halt the renewal of the Kiribati-Soviet Union fishery agreement. However, it could not obstruct the Vanuatu-Soviet Union fishery agreement. It is widely believed that the Soviet Union wants more fish.

Japan and the United States have abandoned their intention to dispose of nuclear wastes in the Pacific. France, however, is still continuing with her nuclear testing at the Muroroa atoll. The South Pacific Nuclear Free Zone Treaty (Rarotonga Treaty) came into force in December 1986, but France and the United States have no intention of signing the Protocol of the Treaty. Also, the Melanesian countries are not willing to sign the Rarotonga Treaty because they believe that the treaty is not effective enough to prevent nuclear vessels from entering their territorial seas.

As far as the motive behind the Fijian coup de'etat is concerned, we surmise that the leader of the coup wanted to stop the Labor/FNP Coalition government's move to align with the Melanesian countries whose foreign policies favored joining the nonaligned movement and oppose the ANZUS strategic cooperation.

Be that as it may, we would like to consider economic vulnerability in the next section, setting aside political vulnerability, although both vulnerabilities are intricately connected.

Development and economic self-reliance: meaning of self-reliance

Every Pacific island country has its own development plan, and economic independence or self-reliance is proclaimed as the objective of all development plans.

One can readily note the phrase "to move toward true economic independence and self-reliance" among the objectives of Western Samoa's Fifth Development Plan, 1985-1987. In the Preamble of the Papua New Guinean Constitution one will find the provision "to be politically and economically independent, and our economy basically self-reliant" inserted as the third national goal.

Even the smallest independent country, Tuvalu, has the phrase "to establish economic policies consistent with the achievement of the National objective of self-reliance" in its development plan, although the planners recognize that the plan has to be carried out totally with overseas capital aid.

We are reminded of the critical words of Ron Crocombe some years ago: "Self-reliance is what existed before contact with the industrial societies. We talk double-talk when we say that we want self-reliance."[3]

We cannot fully agree with Crocombe's definition of self-reliance as subsistence, and we would like to give our interpretation of the real meaning of economic self-reliance in the present age of interdependence. However, before attempting a definition of economic self-reliance, we have to examine the different meanings of "economic independence." In the West Samoan Fifth Development Plan, there is a sentence referring to true economic independence and self-reliance.

Some observers recommend the "Zen economy" strategy or zero economic growth as a means to achieve economic independence. Zen economy calls for living within limited means and adjusting aspirations to match possible results. Zen economy might be a typical pattern of economic independence: investments would be determined by domestic savings; government spendings by domestic revenues; import expenditures, by export earnings; and no foreign aid at all.

If such is to be the understanding of economic independence, Pacific island leaders will never be able to adopt the Zen economy strategy. Island leaders will have to satisfy the rising aspirations of their people caused by their exposure to changing patterns of life. Crocombe's opinion, that "self-reliance is really subsistence" has almost the same connotation as Zen economy.

Another reason for our dislike for the term "economic independence" is rather psychological. This term reminds us of the notorious concept of "autarky," which was widely practiced by the so-called Axis powers to disguise their territorial ambitions. For instance, the Japanese concept of "Greater East-Asia Coprosperity Sphere" was directed to the region, wherein Japan expected to build a vast empire and to achieve a completely self-sufficient economic sphere. As you know, the autarkic strategies of the Axis powers led to the Second World War. Undoubtedly, autarky was a form of aggressive protectionist strategy, too.

Let us return to the question of economic self-reliance. Te'o I. Fairbairn, a distinguished Samoan economist, warned the island countries that commitment to accelerated development programs has led them to become even more dependent on aid and more vulnerable than hitherto. He recommended that the island countries become more selective in their approach toward foreign aid projects and avoid a "take everything" attitude. [4]

Furthermore, Fairbairn asserted that aid dependent development has lessened in some degree the extent to which the island countries can control and manage their own destinies. The need to reconcile this effect with the widely held development objectives of achieving a greater degree of economic self-reliance has never been squarely satisfied.

We are convinced that "economic self-reliance" is an antonym of "economic vulnerability." When an island country loses control over its own economic destiny, it then has to fall into a state of "economic vulnerability."

As to the substance of "economic vulnerability," we have an interesting analysis by economists engaged in the Pacific Islands Studies Program at the University of Hawaii. They use six key criteria (constraints) to analyze the economic vulnerabilities of Pacific island countries. The six criteria are (1) foreign aid dependency; (2) diversity of exports; (3) food substitutability; (4) dependency on imported fuel; (5) fiscal integrity; and (6) political constraints. Neither the per capita GNP nor the balance of trade is used as a criterion by them.

Comparing Western Samoa with American Samoa, let us ask the question as to which is more vulnerable economically?

As far as the per capita GNP is concerned, American Samoa appears to enjoy a much higher GNP than Western Samoa. According to the SPC's statistics, the per capita GNP of American Samoa was U.S. $ 3,442 in 1980 and that of Western Samoa was U.S. $ 723 . As to the balance of trade, in contrast to chronically deficit Western Samoa, American Samoa has continued to enjoy a surplus every year.

The economists at the University of Hawaii, however, pointed out that American Samoa is the most vulnerable country of the two. According to the composite index of the six criteria used by them, American Samoa is ranked fifteenth among the fifteen Pacific countries analyzed. In contrast, Western Samoa is the fifth least vulnerable country, and the composite ranking of Western Samoa is the same with the fourth least vulnerable, Fiji.

The economists conclude that Tonga appears to be the most economically self-reliant among the fifteen Pacific island countries. Additionally, it is the least vulnerable to external economic forces although the per capita GNP of Tonga is lower than that of Western Samoa, and Tonga's balance of trade is chronically deficit ridden.

Examining the above-mentioned analyses, we have to assume that "economic self-reliance" means the ability to control one's own economic destiny. To control one's own destiny, every Pacific island country must have the ability to plan and execute development projects, match changes to the structures of the economy, and reallocate resources, given institutional, organizational, and labor force problems. They call it the economy's "absorptive capacity."

At the Second Pacific Island Conference at Rarotonga, in August 1985, Rodney V. Cole, assistant executive director of the Development Studies Center, Australian National University, read a paper titled "Planning for Pacific Societies of the 21st Century." He cautioned against development plans that are simply rhetorical and those that are merely "begging bowls" or "shopping lists" to be presented to donor nations and agencies. He stressed that development plans must accommodate the concerns of local communities and that consultations with the affected people are crucial if the plans are to reflect their needs. Local administrative bodies can play a vital role in gathering the opinions of the people, and this in turn will make people feel that they are participating in shaping their own destinies.

Cole concluded that the most important aspect of any development plan is the will of the people to succeed in controlling and shaping their own destinies. "If the will to succeed exists, success must surely follow."

At the same conference, I. Q. Lasaga, secretary to the cabinet, Fijian Prime Minister's Department, read a paper titled "Government Policy and the Destiny of the Pacific Islands." He wrote:

> Development is a process of change, modification, and adjustment in the pattern of life and the manner of doing t hings. . . .For the Pacific islands it means a mutual accommodation between the old and the new to meet the demands of the present and the future. Such an approach will enable islanders to influence the course of their futures, although they might not be able to completely control their destinies.

Lasaga's paper represents the attitude of the Pacific island countries in contrast to the aid donors represented by Rodney V. Cole.

Lasaga's rather diffident remark represents the Pacific island leaders' uneasiness about the possible aid-induced erosion of the recipient islanders' will to control their own destinies. By the same token, the planner of Western Samoa's Fourth Development Plan warned of the least tangible long-run disadvantages of aid, which mean "thrift, effort and enterprise are devalued by too heavy an inflow of unearned resources, whether from migrants or from aid donors."

We must emphasize here that the meaning of economic "self-reliance" is the people's will and ability to manage and control their own destinies, even under conditions of aid-dependent development. The meaning of "genuine" development must be defined as the development process that will not bring about aid-induced erosion of the people's will to manage and control their own destinies.

To finalize the discussion on economic self-reliance, we have to refer to the concepts of regional cooperation. Because of its geographic size, population, and natural and human resources endowment, there are various constraints that hinder an individual country's efforts to control its own destiny.

To project and implement development plans that entail several sectors and that depend on economies of size, such as fisheries surveillance, transportation, telecommunications, and higher education, individual island countries would derive greater benefits through cooperation and by joining some regional institutions that promise better results through consolidation.

Dr. Fairbairn included industrial planning, tourism, and basic agricultural and agro-based industry research as possible areas for future regional cooperation. And he warned as follows:

> Some of these are difficult areas where a regional approach can easily flounder as it comes up against national interest and unjustifiable inequity in the sharing of possible benefits. The test of economic and financial feasibility as opposed to technical viability must also be faced. Clearly, there is a need to understand and appreciate the limits to regional economic cooperation.[5]

We would like to end the discussion by quoting the opinion of Ronald Crocombe: "As a percentage of the total, the scope for regional solutions is small--but it is nevertheless a particularly important element in the total package of national and international options."

As to the PBCC, Crocombe indicated that the concept has considerable significance for the islands countries. His suggestion for the island countries was "to decide whether they would be better off to join a Pacific Basin grouping, or whether they would achieve better results working as a bloc."

Notes

1.   Barrie MacDonald, "Decolonization and Beyond, *Journal of Pacific History,* July 1986.

2. *Far Eastern Economic Review, Asia 1982 Yearbook.*

3. "Power, Politics, and Rural People" in *The Road Out: Rural Development in the Solomon Islands, USP,* 1981.

4. "Economic Forces: Constraints and Potentials" in *Foreign Forces in Pacific Politics, USP,* 1983.

5. Te'o I. Fairbairn, "Island Economics: Studies from the South Pacific," *USP,* 1985, p. 86.

Appendix C

Project on the Pacific Region: A Proposal for the Formation of Education Relationship Networks

Background

Responsibility for the development of education and communications development for the resources of the South Pacific islands must be shared by the nations involved. Through such cooperation, many advantages may be shared by all.

During July 1986 a study mission, led by Toshio Kosuge together with five other professors from the University of Electro-Communications (UEC), toured Fiji, Tonga, Western Samoa, and American Samoa.

The purposes of the tour were to determine ways to enrich the curriculum of a recently initiated course on "International Technical Cooperation" offered at UEC, and find methods to cooperate with higher educational institutes in the South Pacific region.

Observations were made with reference to the present status of the following areas:

1. education for science and technology;
2. telecommunication and information processing;
3. telecommunication facilities and their development plan; and
4. the regional economic development plan.

This appendix was prepared by Toshio Kosuge and Masatomo Tonaka, University of Electro-Communications, Tokyo.

This fact-finding mission was enthusiastically received and aided by a number of persons, including Ronald Crocombe of the University of the South Pacific (USP), E. J. Wilkinson, in charge of the South Pacific Telecommunication Development Programme (SPTDP) and his staff, the common carrier staff of FINTEL, and numerous professionals interviewed. The detailed results of the mission's observations have been published in a report.[1]

The mission recognizes the distinctive feature of the region, which is the diversity of ethnic groups and cultures developed as a result of island isolation and low population density.

Many people of the region are eager to receive education in order to cope with this diversity. There are elementary schools on many small islands. USP, managed by twelve nations in the region, provides opportunities for higher education for students of the Laucala and Alafua campuses, as well as extension services using the ATS-1 satellite (while it was still operating), which were directed by Marjorie Crocombe for students living on remote islands.

Many persons interviewed expressed their wish to introduce computers for education and business improvements.

The mission determined that there are only a few direct telecommunication circuits established between the island nations surveyed, since many islands have no domestic telecommunication facilities or even electricity.

SPTDP plans to improve regional communication facilities by

- digitalization of domestic trunks;
- utilization of INTELSAT's transponder for interregional communications;
- consideration of PACSTAR, to be owned by TRT, a U.S. company, and Papua New Guinea; and
- trial of a submarine optical fiber cable in Cook Islands.

SPTDP expects AUSAT, an Australian domestic satellite to be operated in the K3 band, so that it can be utilized for TV relay.[2,3,4,5] A TV program will be transmitted to Fiji from Australia.

The South Pacific Bureau for Economic Cooperation (SPEC) recognizes the need for an efficient system of communication and information to unite the people of the South Pacific islands.

The mission determined that one of the most important projects for the development of the region is the expansion of higher education resources to establish, manage, operate, and maintain information and communications facilities.

Existing proposals

A satellite communications system is vital to improving international communication services. INTELSAT, established in 1964, is a single global satellite system. It provides worldwide satellite communication services with its universal fare rate. INTELSAT has made many contributions over the past twenty years toward the development of international communications in both developed and developing countries. Additional demands for new satellite systems have evolved to meet the needs for increasing volume of information and new services.

To meet these demands, INTELSAT provides new facilities, such as low-cost earth stations, and new services, including VISTA, IBS, and so on, especially for thin-route users.[6]

In recent years, our ideas have been proposed aiming at the improvement of information and communications in the Pacific region. Two of them are designing for non-INTELSAT systems, and one is applied to INTELSAT's new development program.

Figure C.1
An example of coverage of PRSC

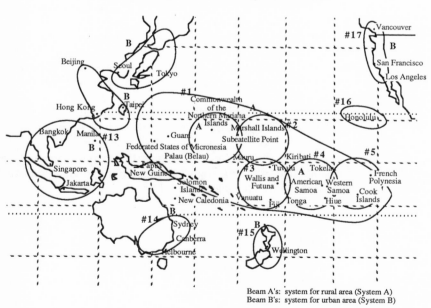

Beam A's: system for rural area (System A)
Beam B's: system for urban area (System B)

The Pacific regional satellite communication systems:[7,8] PRSCS

These systems have been proposed by Nozomu Takasaki of Misubishi Electric Corporation. The outline of the systems follows:

In the Pacific region, the need for various telecommunications increases every year. This proposal presents two main points. The first aims at the improvement of communication systems between remote islands and rural areas. The other covers high-speed data and video transmissions between major cities.

The satellite beam coverage shown in Figure C.1 is presented as a model as well as the technical restrictions on one geostationary satellite. ASEAN countries are expanding their domestic communication networks by leasing the PALAPA transponder from Indonesia.

The possible launch date of the satellite is between 1990 and 1995. The construction of the model system is to be completed by 1992. The service life of the satellite is predicted to be seven years (end of life in 1999).

Traffic forecasts

a. Traffic forecasts in remote islands and capitals of the Pacific region (hereafter called rural traffic) are presented in this study. The method of forecasting traffic is to determine rural traffic in various countries based on per capita GNP, telephone density, and rural and remote islands population. It is forecast that the average rural telephone density in the whole Pacific islands areas in 1999 (end of the satellite life) will be about 230 Erlangs during peak transmission hours.

b. Traffic forecasts for high speed digital communications between major cities. Traffic during the lifetime of the satellite, from 1990 to 1999, is projected in four categories of services among the major cities of the Pacific region. These will be high speed data transmissions over 48 kbps, high-speed facsimile, teleconference, and telephone services for selected neighboring countries.

Concept of the System

The study was made to determine the most effective telecommunication system for the South Pacific islands. This design consists of System A for the remote and rural areas and System B for major cities.

System A (see Figure C.1) will be established for remote communications through a small earth station with a 4-5 meter diameter antenna in an oval beam (#6 in Figure C.1), which will cover Pacific Ocean islands. The earth station and terminals will be connected by VHF radios. With this system, TV or radio programs will be distributed to the above mentioned small earth stations through spot beams (#1-5) and retransmitted on the ground.

If a high-grade earth station is used, the oval beam will be powerful enough to reach Honolulu and Australia. Public communications from major cities covered by the beam are shown in Figure C.1 (#11-17). High speed signals, such as video conferences and data transmissions, involve many restrictions through the conventional communication network with the domestic terrestrial system. By installing a small earth station on the user site, the high speed signals can be transmitted directly through the satellite. At the end of 1994, the estimated volume of telecommunications traffic would require two of the one-ton geostationary satellites.

The satellite broadcast service system in the Asian and Oceanian region: AOSAT[9,10]

The broadcasting satellite system was designed as a technical study by Dr. Tadashi Iida, Masaaki Shimada of Radio Research Laboratories, Ministry of Posts and Telecommunications, and their colleagues and engineers from Nippon Electric Corporation (NEC). This design was presented at PTC '85.

Table C.1.
An example of broadcast system parameters

Country	East longitude	Beam number	Beamwidth	Transmit power
PAK	73	1	2.5	30.4
NPL	85	1	2.5	30.4
BHU	90	1	2.5	30.4
BGD	90	2	2.5	30.4
BRM	96	2	2.5	30.4
MLD	74	3	2.1	21.5
CLM	80	3	2.1	21.5
SLM	160	4	2.1	21.5
NRU	167	5	2.1	21.5
LOR	172	5	2.1	21.5
TUV	178	5	2.1	21.5
VIT	168	6	2.1	21.5
FJI	178	6	2.1	21.5
TON	184	6	2.1	21.5
SMO	188	6	2.1	21.5

Satellite broadcast countries

Countries selected have less than 4 hours per day on the network of TV broadcasting or have a very low spread rate of TV sets. Countries whose policies might limit TV broadcasting, are not independent, or have their own broadcast satellite are not offered services. Thus seven Asian and eight Oceanian countries were selected as shown in Table C.1

The coverage of the satellite is indicated in Figure C.2.

Figure C.2.
An example of coverage

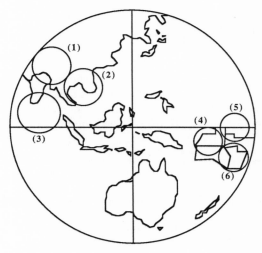

Configuration of the on-board transponder

This satellite broadcast system requires an on-board transponder as shown in Figure C.3. This transponder will be able to broadcast the Asian or Oceanian region.

A typical channel plan is shown in Figure C.4 with channels shared by the Asian and Oceanian countries. Their longitudinal difference is approximately 90 degrees, which correspond to a time difference of six hours. Neighboring downlink channels use orthogonal polarization to prevent channel-to-channel interference.

Figure C.3
An example of transponder

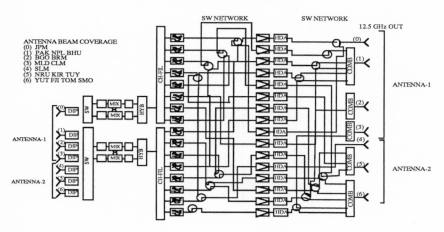

Space segment parameters

Table C.2 is an example of the satellite parameters of its space segment.

Table C.2
An example of space segment parameters

Satellite bus	Hughes HS376 equivalent
Launch vehicle	PAM-D class
Satellite life	7 years or more
Orbital locations	125 degrees east longitude
Eclipse capacity	100% (2 X 2.895 Ah MiCd batteries)
Satellite dry weight	508 kg
Solar panel capability	954 Watts (EDL Summer Solstice)
Satellite antenna and attitude control	Beam pointing accuracy 0.2 deg./0.05 deg. (without/with tracking)
Mission weight	107 kg (transponder) 29 kg (2 X 80 cm diameter antennas)
Mission Power	730 Watts
Transponder	Uplink (14 DHz band) 8 channels from Japan and 8 channels from broadcast countries Downlink (12.5 GHz band) 1 channel to Japan and 8 channels to broadcast countries.

Figure C.4
An example of channel plan

UPLINK   DOWNLINK   ASIA   OCEANIA

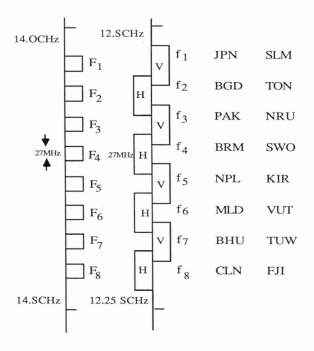

Data communication and information exchanging network: ASTINFONET[11]

The ASTINFONET was developed by Norman Abramson of the University of Hawaii. To this design INTELSAT would assist in the formation of this network.[12] The network would be used for the scientific data and for the technical and cultural information exchange needed by many institutions in Asia and Oceania. The following proposal was presented to UNESCO.

Needs

Information exchange needs in Asia and the Pacific are numerous, and the cost of failing to meet those needs, both in human and economic terms, is considerable. The proposed network could provide the equipment and system through which a number of social, cultural, and educational institutions within the region could enhance the delivery of their programs. The following outline presents a few areas in which this network system could be applied:

libraries and resource centers
agriculture
health care and health education
education
development projects
management of resources
disaster warning and relief
regional cultural events
conservation of energy and time

Applications

Some applications possible with a low-cost data communications network are

a.   messaging and telecommunication services;
b.   electronic mail;
c.   document identification and delivery service;
d.   collection and distribution of data from remote sensing units; and
e.   the exchange of data between participating centers.

All of these potential applications will be considered for inclusion in the system. Appropriate applications could differ for each of the pilot user-participant organizations. The technology should remain flexible enough to accommodate such variety.

Technical approaches

Considerable thought has been given to the telecommunication needs of developing countries. A number of plans and potential resources have already been outlined or offered. It would be wise to review some of the more significant of these developments before proceeding to outline the parameters and potentials of the pilot network.

Pan-Pacific information network:[13] PPI-net

The PPI-Net has been proposed by Shoichi Noguchi and Yoshiaki Nemoto of Tohoku University, Japan, aiming at the establishment of an international human-human network. The paper mentioning the PPI-Net was presented to the Asia-Pacific Satellite Communication Symposium held in Tokyo. According to the paper, the utilization for academic and/or educational purposes and the realization in three phases of the PPI-Net are as follows (Note: In this subsection "we" indicates Noguchi and Nemoto, authors of the paper referred to.).

Utilization of the network

The following objectives may be achieved using the academic information network over the Asia-Oceania regime: long-distance classrooms, educational information exchange, sharing of educational software, collection and exchange of various types of data, document exchange, reference of various data bases, on-line scientific computation, utilization of various application software, utilization of various data bases, electric mail, long distance meetings, and videotex.

Phase 1: Post-ATS-1 network

Considering the achievement and the present status of the Asia and Oceania networks for academic purposes, it is most urgent and important to construct a network that is of the same level as our ATS-1 network. In the first phase of network construction, we propose to build the network with the same level of function as in ATS-1. ATS-1 networks had many earth stations and were of great help to several users. So, given a new satellite of a capability similar to the ATS-1, we can restart network activities and make additional plans. It is important to mention that the success of the ATS-1 network stemmed from the possibility of free access to the satellite and low-cost earth stations. So while planning this phase of the network, these factors will certainly be kept in mind.

In phase 1 of the network, voice communication and slow speed data transmission (several kbps) will be available. It will also be necessary to have several voice channels.

Currently, the post ATS-1 plan by NASA is eagerly awaited, and our country is also looking forward to contributing to the project.

Phase 2: Computer network with small satellite channel

The utilization of computer systems for educational and research purposes will increase rapidly in Asian and Oceanian countries in the near future. So at this stage, it will become very important to realize a uniform environment for the utilization of computer resources for academic purposes. At the initial stage of this phase, it will become possible to have access to the huge database stored in developed countries from anywhere in the region using this network.

In this network, packet switching will be used, and its data transmission rate will be 9.6 kbps-64 kbps. In the future, cheaper earth stations are expected. Also the international standard communication protocol will be fixed, and many communication devices will be made using the latest in IC technology. All this is expected to lead to remarkable progress in network design and development. As for the satellite of this network, it is possible to consider leasing the INTELSAT satellite. Nevertheless, we strongly believe, as ATS-1 networks have shown, utilization of a nonprofit satellite leads to very strong network activities.

Projecting the development of satellite communication technology into the future, it may be said that the satellite used in this phase of the network will be a multibeam satellite of Ku-band and that small size earth stations will be used in the packet switching mode. It is also important to retain the voice communication in this network along with packet transmission. To allow an equal opportunity utilization, a kind of reservation multiaccess method may be employed.

Phase 3: Multi-media computer network system

This network is the development of the phase 2 network. Every kind of function needed for academic activity will be available at this stage. Information will be converted into digital signals and will be exchanged through the integrated satellite data communication network. Finally, the international academic ISDN will be established. The academic ISDN should be upwardly compatible with the future international ISDN.

A proposal for the formation of the South Pacific education relationship network: SUPERNET

Progress of the Asia-Pacific region will surely be increasingly promoted through formation of a closely cooperative relationship network between nations of the South Pacific region and Japan, in addition to the existing relations. Satellite systems and information networks introduced in the previous section must stand as the tight framework of the new relationship network.

The SUPERNET network proposed here is, as a small mesh of the huge relational network, aiming at resources development with particular reference to the information and communications field among the universities in the South Pacific region and UEC. A conceptional schema is shown in Figure C.5.

The outline of services is

a. International graduate course in information and telecommunications (IGCIT) in UEC;
b. Department of communication systems (DCS) in the South Pacific region;
c. Data/information exchanging network and data base; and
d. Multimedia distance education system.

The enrollment of foreign students, dispatching teachers to foreign universities and institutions, academic data/information exchange, and the improvement of education and training will be augmented by the utilization of SUPERNET.

Figure C.5.
A conceptional schema of the SUPERNET

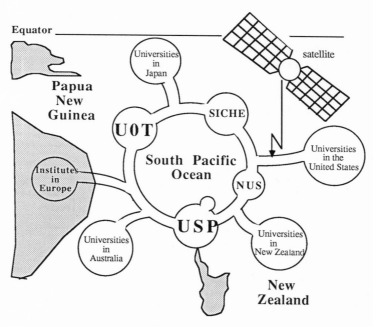

Provision of an international graduate course in information and telecommunications technology at UEC

A new course to be offered by UEC will be proposed to the Ministry of Education and Culture. This class will be called "The International Course in

Information and Telecommunications" (ICIT). The information presented in this class will guide students to develop resources exchange.

There is an international consensus that information and telecommunication networks are indispensable infrastructures for national development. Such networks are urgently needed in developing countries for the exchange of information and technology.

In order to promote mutual understanding and the exchange of students and researchers between the South Pacific region and Japan, it would be appropriate for UEC to initiate these programs as soon as possible.

UEC, with experienced teachers and resources in the field of information and telecommunications would like to establish international courses at the graduate level for students from developing countries. There will be about 20 instructors for the courses, including professors, associate professors, visiting professors, and technicians. About 20 non-Japanese students will be received each year. All guidance and lectures will be given in English.

Subjects taught will include:
- Information theory
- Information processing
- Information transmission
- Systems engineering
- Telecommunication systems
- Artificial intelligence
- Information management
- International technical cooperation
- International law and policy of communications
- Education technology
- Others

Research subjects will include:
- International information and telecommunication systems
- Integrated services digital networks (ISDN)
- Trans border data flow
- International value added networks
- International communications
- Machine translation
- International development planning
- Transfer of technology
- Other

Establishment of a Department of Communication Systems (DCS): in the South Pacific region

Highly trained information and telecommunications engineers will be assigned to the DCS. The need for advanced training of this department would be provided by Japanese official development aid (ODA), through a qualified university in the South Pacific region.

The DCS will seek to meet the needs of a more technologically advanced society. DCS will provide training for engineers to become highly proficient in electronics, telecommunications, and computer skills. Student entry level would be determined by previous academic training.

Master of Engineering and Doctor of Engineering degrees can be offered at UEC in Japan. A student who graduated with a Bachelor of Engineering Degree from DCS or another school in the South Pacific region could be enrolled in the graduate school of UEC with priority. These students would be able to enroll in the ICIT program described above.

Development of academic data/information exchange network with data base: Mini-Net

These networks that have been planned by Abramson and Noguchi as mentioned in the previous section will necessarily need a large budget and enough time to develop successfully. The Mini-Net presented here is to be realized easily utilizing VSAT[13] among USP, UOT, and UEC. Data/information as well as educational materials relating to the information and communications field can be exchanged among these three universities through INTELSAT or another appropriate satellite.

The Mini-Net may be viewed as a regional and specific trial for the larger network mentioned above. We can find a prototype of the Mini-Net in the USP-Net that is currently used between Laucala campus and the extension centers for the extension services through INTELSAT under its SHARE Project. The USP-Net is going to realize data exchange between their personal computers located in Laucala campus and their centers. USP plans to develop a kind of data base for data exchanging.[14]

The Mini-Net will soon need a sufficient data base to cope with its activities so that the latter must be equipped with the Net at the beginning of development.

An approach to multi-media distance education systems

Audio-visual (AV) educational material, that is, AV communication media, can be categorized into four types: visual linguistic (VL), visual nonlinguistic (VN), audible linguistic (AL), and audible nonlinguistic (AN). Each type of medium presents its own characteristics as shown in Table C.3. [15]

Table C.3
Audio-visual media categorized into four types

	Visible: V	Audible: A
Lingistic: L	**VL** Letter, writing, figure, table, equation, numerical formula, etc. suitable to describe, prove, induce, deduce, reason things and phenomena.	**AL** Word, conversation, speech, narration, reading, lecture, etc. adequate to tell a story, fable, history, to explain, persuade, make one pay attention, express one's feeling, emotion, sentiment, passion and so on.
Non-Linguistic:N	Graph, chart, diagram, picture, photograph, illustration, visuals, computer graphics, etc. appropriate to present image, shape, color, one's expression, geography, landscape and their motion or change. **VN**	Song, music to make one gay, sad, sublime, mysterious atmosphere, associate or remind something. Sounds proper to the things and phenomena. **AN**

We cannot recognize AV educational material separately as a medium in itself and the information carried by the medium. The amount of intelligence that a student will store internally after absorbing educational material depends on his former experiences and cultural background. Therefore, the effect of such educational material can be maximized through the appropriate selection of the types of medium that compose the material as well as the volume of contents to be carried by each type of medium according to what is to be informed. The multimedia are to be produced through the most appropriate combination of these types of medium according to the educational information to be presented to the students.

The transmission of VN media, especially in the case of TV programs, requires wide-band communication channels. "Wide" is a synonym for "expensive" in the telecommunication world.

To avoid large expenses in transmission, the following procedure may be adoptable:

a.   Video tapes or disks on which VN and AN media are recorded, and floppy disks on which VL media are recorded are to be transported previously to distant recipient sites. Audio tapes on which AL media are recorded should also undergo the same procedure, if necessary.

b.   The teacher can dispatch VN and AN media controlling the video tape/disk player loading the transported tape/disk on it through telephone circuit being connected there. He can also present VL media by controlling micro computer loading on the floppy disk.

c.   His voice for lectures can be transmitted through the telephone circuit directly, or he can present lectures by controlling the audio tape recorder on which the audio tape, transported previously, is

d.   The teacher can invite any questions or opinions from remote students through the telephone circuit.

Multimedia educational material mentioned above can be produced using the production design in Figure C.6.[16]

Figure C.6
Multimedia production system

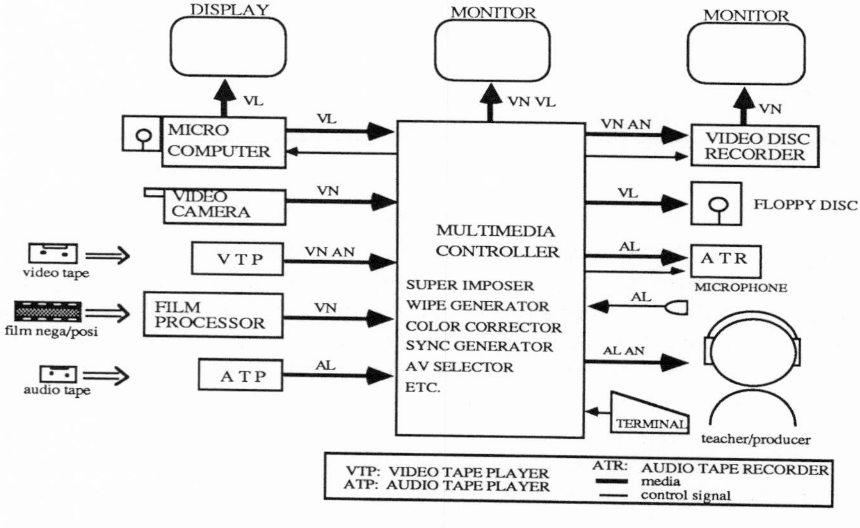

The design of the distance education system that will allow the procedure indicated above is shown in Figure C.7.[17]

Figure C.7
Multimedia distance education system

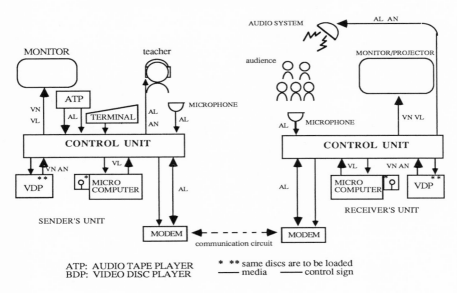

ATP: AUDIO TAPE PLAYER   * ** same discs are to be loaded
BDP: VIDEO DISC PLAYER   —— media   —— control sign

Equipment for production and presentation of the multimedia educational materials is available. However, materials themselves have to be produced by the nation or in the institute where education will be offered. Mutual cooperation for developing the materials and exchanging materials produced is necessary for the success of international distance education.

Conclusion

Considering the distinctive features of the region, the diversity of ethnic groups and cultures developed as the result of island isolation, and the low population density, there exists a need for extending the range of communication in the South Pacific islands. In order to overcome the low level of information and telecommunication, it will be very effective to have satellite telecommunication networks as mentioned before.

SUPERNET, proposed above, could play a great role in developing education and research for building cooperating networks among institutions concerned about the South Pacific region. Establishment of a Department of Communication Systems: (DCS) in this region could be a node of the network and could contribute to the education of a number of able students in the field of information and telecommunications in the region.

PRSCS, AOSAT, ASTINFONET, or PPI-Net, introduced above, could promote cultural exchanges and mutual understanding as well as unification of the region by supporting the SUPERNET. AOSAT, especially, make it possible for the South Pacific region to have the University of the Air with the establishment of the educational program production facilities and ground stations of the satellite broadcasting system.

There will be a great opportunity for international cooperation among academic institutions in Asia and Oceania to establish facilities and programs. These institutions are, for example, USP, UOT, SICHE, the Agriculture Extension Center of Kasetsart University in Thailand, ETV of SEAMEO-RECSAM in Malaysia, the Multimedia Training Center in Indonesia, JICA Okinawa International Center, the University of the Air in Japan, and so on.

The authors of this paper present these proposals to the academic institutions of the South Pacific region in order to request assistance from the Japanese official development aid, (ODA). These must be considered carefully by both the South Pacific countries and other countries to implement international cooperation.

It would be advisable for academic institutions in the region to begin immediate action for international cooperation with UEC, such as:

    a.   Survey for a feasibility study for establishing or strengthening engineering training with academic institutions in the region;

    b.   Experiment of the Mini-Net and provision of data base

    c.   Development of multimedia educational materials

Notes

1.   Toshio Kosuge, Masatomo Tanaka et al., "The Report of UEC Study Mission on Education for Telecommunications and Information Technology in the South Pacific Region" (in Japanese), Report of University of Electro-Communications, 37::2 (February 1987).

2.   E. J. Wilkinson, "System and Hardware Options for Digital Telecommunication Networks in the South Pacific," Proceedings of the PTC 1985, January 1985.

3.   Wilkinson, "Satellite Communication for Development," - The South Pacific Telecommunications Development Programme, AIBD/IIC Seminar, Kuala Lumpur, Malaysia, June 1986.

4.   *South Pacific Telecommunication Development Programme Planning Report,* South Pacific Bureau for Economic Cooperation (SPEC), Suva, Fiji, April, 1986.

5.   Wilkinson, "Planning the Use of Satellite Transmission within the South Pacific Telecommunications Development Programme," Proceedings of the PTC 1987, January 1987.

6. J. N. Pelton and R. A. Lemus, "INTELSAT's Plans for the Pacific Region," Proceedings of the PTC 1986, January 1986.
7. Nozumu Takasaki, "A Study on the Pacific Regional Satellite Communication System," Proceedings of the PTC 1983, January 1983.
8. Nozomu Takasaki, "The Pacific Regional Satellite Communication System," Proceedings of TIDE-200, Tokyo, November 1985.
9. Takashi Iida, Masaaki Shimada et al., "A Study on the Broadcasting Services in the Asian and Oceanian Regions Using a Satellite System," (in Japanese), Association for Promotion of International Cooperation (APIC), June 1984.
10. Tadashi Iida, Masaaki Shimada et al., "A Study on the Satellite Broadcast Service System in the Asian and Oceanian Regions," Proceedings of the PTC 1985, January 1985.
11. Norman Abramson, "Data Communication and Information Exchange Network (ASTINFONET)," UNESCO Technical Report, PR/1984-1985/7 1. 3, June 1985.
12. Abramson, "Data Communication and Information Exchange Network."

13. Shoichi Noguchi and Yoshiaki Nemoto, "The Conception of an Academic Information Network for the Pan-Pacific Region," Procedings of the Asia-Pacific Satellite Communication Symposium, Tokyo, April 1987.
14. Joseph Freitag, Jr., "Very Small Aperture Terminals (VSAT)," Proceedings of the PTC 1987, January 1987.
15. Masatomo Tanaka, "A Study of a Cross Cultural Engineering Education Process Supported by Audio-visual Media," *Journal of EESEA*, 16:2 (September 1986).
16. Masatomo Tanaka, Toyoshi Arisawa et al., "A Study of a Multi-media Distance Education System," (in Japanese), IECEJ Technical Report, ET86-88, November 1986.
17. Tanaka, Arisawa et al., "Study of a Multimedia Distance Education System."

Appendix D

Highlights of On-Line Discussion for the Global Community Forum, 1987

One month before the in-person Global Community Forum '87 in Western Samoa, APIC started to learn the practicability of a new type of consensus-making system, that is, the computer conferencing system.

For this challenge we utilized three computer networks. They are "TWICS" (Two-Way Information and Communication System) in Tokyo, Japan, "The Source" in Virginia, U.S.A., and "Unison" in Ohio, U.S.A.

We opened an on-line version of the Global Community Forum on each network and these three networks were linked with one another to share all messages. This means anyone who could hook up with one of these networks could join the conference and exchange opinions and questions regardless of time and distance.

The following are the highlights for each session:

Session 1:   "Pacific Economic Development"

Paul: I would just like to throw out the query of whether it is possible for a less-developed country to accept aid (money, advice, technology) from outside without compromising its autonomy. I, myself, don't know. What do you think?

Milo: I think there are "possible safeguards" that might help in maintaining whatever degree of autonomy is possible when you choose to participate in a world economy.

   But one of the points I was attempting to highlight was that our island neighbors have been, historically, forced to participate in that same "world economy" as slaves or parasites, for the most part, and I think there is sufficient evidence that it need not, of necessity, be that way today.

What I mean is that, through the use of various technologies (such as communications; alternative energy sources; clean buildings/manufacturing methods and materials; controlled and planned tourism, and so on), as well as increased intellectual and face-to-face participation as an equally responsible and equally supported member in a larger community, it is certainly possible that the various peoples of the Pacific might directly experience a greater degree of autonomy than they have to date.

I do not think, personally, that there is much room in our world for true independence. I do think, however, that we can have self-directed interdependence.

One possible starting point in this topic might be the question, "What are the tools, processes, information, and resources (human and otherwise) that would help to guarantee self-directed interdependence for a local community or economy involved in an economic development project?"

Paul (Paul Henriques) is an American working as a translator for some banks in Tokyo, and Milo (Milo Parsons) is also an American working in Tokyo as a computer consultant and is known as an expert on Ponape

Session 2: "Pacific Market Condition"

Sumpei: As far as Japan is concerned, the first serious interest in the Pacific region as a whole was taken under the leadership of the late prime minister, Masayoshi Ohira, who advocated the Pacific-rim Cooperation Initiative in the 1970s. A study group was organized in the beginning of 1979 to further develop this initiative with Dr. Saburo Ohkita, former minister of foreign affairs, presiding. This group submitted its final report in May 1980, just one month before Mr. Ohira passed away.

Readers of this report will be struck by its vagueness and abstract expressions, which were intentional, because the whole topic was extremely sensitive politically. Thus the authors of the report carefully avoided even defining the range of the Pacific-rim area: they could neither exclude nor include Mainland China, Taiwan, North Korea, or Vietnam, for instance. Should the Soviet Union be included in the Pacific rim? If they want to include Latin America, what they should do about Brazil? Is talking only about economic cooperation sufficient? Maybe one should begin gradually with cultural exchanges. Or perhaps one should step further ahead, talking boldly about political integration or collective security, even if in extremely abstract terms. Apparently there was no way to settle these questions at that time. (Professional diplomats then were horrified by the prime minister's idea of picking up the Pacific region as a serious topic of discussion.)

Another interesting thing about this report is that no explicit reference to the so-called Pacific-basin island countries is to be found in it. Most probably, no one paid attention to them at that time. It was only a few years after this report had been published, it seems to me, that Japan began to be somewhat encouraged by the strong interest taken by South Korea and China in this initiative, though most of them do not know how to deal with the Soviet interest in it. Today it is taken for granted (as far as public opinion in Japan is concerned, I guess) that the pan-Pacific region includes both the Pacific-rim and the Pacific basin, of which Korea and China are parts.

Incidentally, South Korea's economic performance is really breath-taking. A few years ago it was wondered if South Korea could pay back all of its external debts to Japan by the end of this century. But today, no one can deny the possibility that all the debts will be paid back by 1990, and Korea will be earning a surplus in its trade with Japan. I, for one, am awaiting for the day when I can buy Korean made personal computers, laser-disk players, and of course automobiles, of good quality and with reasonable prices. Thailand, for that matter, clearly seems to have taken off. I have heard that its export to Japan has been increasing quite rapidly. Now it is hard to recall that there were trade frictions between Thailand and Japan concerning boneless chickens.

Shumpei (Shumpei Kumon) is a professor at the University of Tokyo, his speciality is social systems and general systems theories. He is one of the board members for APIC and joined the second GCF in Malaysia.

Section 3: "Pacific Technology Transfer"

Milo: What is the scope of the term technology transfer as used herein?
          Are we limiting the term to include only "high" tech stuff such as computers, earth stations, and the like or are we also going to deal with the issues of appropriate technology, and the balanced introduction and implementation of socially, economically, and technologically appropriate tools and processes that really do serve the best interests of the local recipient?

Kevin: In regard to your statement about high tech/appropriate tech, I think we should be careful not to confuse the level of "sophistication" with the degree of "appropriateness." In other words, high tech can sometimes be "appropriate," while low tech is sometimes inappropriate.

I realize you were not implying such a simple dichotomy, but often these terms take on a meaning of their own. Hopefully this discussion will include the criteria of "appropriate" and not just the topic of transferring high tech to less developed countries.

Stephan: In my past experience, appropriate technology as a term is only relevant when used in conjunction with the culture and place where it is to be employed. Let me give an example.

In Africa, there is the big problem that scavenging wood for cooking reduces the shrubbery, thereby baring the soil, opening it up for wind induced abrasion, and destroying the small layer of fertile earth. Scientists tried to substitute wood fire stoves through solar ovens.

This seemed to be a very appropriate technology for the Sahara, where there is plenty of sun. But it was not accepted, as people living there were accustomed to cooking inside and usually after sunset. So a solar oven was not functional.

The eventual appropriate technology was the invention of a "thermal can," a heat-storing device, that was heated up in the daytime and then carried with a stick to the hut, where it was used in the evening for cooking.

Kevin: I agree that the term "appropriate technology" is only meaningful when used in the context of a particular culture. Moreover, I think it is also important to look at the developmental aspect of the technology transfer question without a determining view.

It is too easy to look at the Third World countries and assume that the developmental model described by the first world is the one to follow. However, there are many reasons for not following this path. Not only is industrialization ecologically and culturally inappropriate for many countries, but it may not be necessary.

The current fashion is to cite the "coming of the information society" as the step beyond industrialization. Why then should less industrialized societies have to suffer through the same mistakes that industrializing societies made? Likewise, industrialized countries could learn from the application of new technologies in lesser-developed nations. By carefully examining the ways in which new technologies are applied in these contexts, both developed and less-developed nations can benefit.

But the important point here is that we should not assume a linear model of development. Appropriate technology is thus not identified by its "fit" with a "level" of development, but rather by its ability to fulfill locally defined needs and goals.

Kevin (Kevin Barron) is a communications student at the Simon Fraser University in Vancouver, and Stephen (Stephen Meyn) is a German who lives and works in Tokyo as a computer systems engineer.

Session 4: "Pacific Human Resources"

Joichi: Now that I know what human resources infrastructure means, how do you develop this? It seems to me that such "development" would be very difficult without impinging on the cultural needs of these societies. Does "development" include changing the work ethic, culture, mores, and so on?

Stephan: That would be a pretty hard-core approach. I am also rather ignorant on this topic. But I guess that as resources are related to cultural background as well as goals to be done, they are also related to tools available.

A Palauan fisherman wouldn't be able to run the equipment of a deep sea trawler, so it wouldn't accomplish much in the way of resource development to put them together.

This to my opinion is the grossest error in international development methods. Human resources in Third World countries are often not adaptable to the technical solutions. For this reason frequently technical experts are sent to countries to make the technical solutions "work." Any long-term solution is endangered by this practice, as the experts are there only so long.

It seems this is where the human resource debate meets technological debate. The question of which technology allows the existing human resources to be utilized well is the one that might give the best answers to Joichi's questions.

George: Human resources are not people, but people with a context in which they are considered to be resources. I wouldn't feel comfortable defining any context for the Palau fishermen, but I would like to learn from them whether there's anything in our technologies that they might want to use. Not an easy question, and since I don't think I'll go to Palau in the near future, I'd like to discuss issues that closer relate with what I can do something about. Does this topic exclude discussion of what might result from "electronic citizen summitry," of those Pacific "human resources" who do have access to the kind of technology that we use here?

Jefu: I suggest that a concrete goal of this conference might begin building a network of like-minded educators and sponsoring organizations, including schools, of course, and to begin working toward virtual educational opportunities of people in the Pacific region.

The initial problem is goals, because we all have different ones, with some working toward their vision of "economic development" and others, like John Southworth and I, more interested in expanding opportunities for cultural exchange. I attended a conference in Dallas last March (International Informatics Access '87) at which we were attempting to investigate the application of information technology to development. On the last day we broke up into regional groups, and a couple of fellows from India were ready to get down to some serious development talk. They felt that those of us from the United States and Japan and so on were there to help develop their countries. I told one of the guys that my central concern was cultural exchange through providing more opportunities for Japanese people to meet people from other cultures, and that I was not really interested in Indian agricultural development. I said that I felt that once the channels of communication were open, and once the human relationships were initiated, then it would be possible for the people involved to be interested in cooperation with each other for mutual development.

I suggest that the same holds true here. It is nice to say that we are going to work together to improve the economics of certain nations of the Pacific region and that can be reinforced later. They set the precedent and provide concrete models for the future. And, they let us make mistakes now, before we are committed to some expansive implementation, as we fiddle around trying to find the most appropriate technology and approaches to use.

Joichi (Joichi Ito) is a student at the University of Chicago and is known as a ubiquitous telecom freak. George (George Por) is a resident of California and a director for High Lights Research and Publishing, exploring the potentials of Inter-Media (print/electronic/face-to-face) Synergy. And Jefu (Jeffrey Shapard) is an American working for TWICS in Tokyo as a systems operator.

Appendix E

Banking and Business Development

Because I feel that there is more to international cooperation than interest rate adjustment, trade deficits, and their corresponding surpluses, I would like to give you a practical example of cooperation between Germany and countries in the Asia-Pacific region.

First of all, a few words about the Stadtsparkasse Koln. The Stadtsparkasse Koln has been around since 1826. With total assets of over 15 billion DM it is the fourth largest savings bank in West Germany. The German savings banks are essentially regional banks with a corporate clientele of small- and medium-sized companies. In Cologne, the largest city in North Rhine-Westphalia, West Germany's most populous state, we have over 120 branches. In the Cologne area, exports account for more than one third of the total industrial production.

Although the Stadtsparkasse has existed for over 160 years, we are still relatively new to foreign business. The philosophy behind the German savings banks movement has always been to assist our customers in whatever field of business such assistance is needed. A modest amount of foreign business with such rudimentary transactions as foreign exchange, foreign trade financing, and documentary business was started over 25 years ago. However, as customer demand for more international business services

This appendix was prepared by Fritz Hermanns.

increased, so we were able to tailor our response in accordance with their wishes. Through the EEC, Europe has become a single market to such an extent that "exporting abroad" now means going somewhat farther afield--and why not?

This is where the link with the Asian and Pacific rim countries comes in and will help to explain why I, as a representative of a large German regional bank, am speaking to you today. Our home market has become saturated, so our customers are looking for new business partners. The Asia-Pacific region, as the world's fastest growing economic region, seemed to us to be an area in which we could anticipate our corporate customers' future needs and help them find suitable import and export outlets. Of course, we are fully aware that some Asian countries have been hit by the decline in world market prices for raw materials and agricultural produce, owing in part to protectionist measures of Western countries. But we have great confidence in the potential and the vigor of their economies and their ability to master temporary set-backs.

As the distances involved here are of a greater magnitude than those of our European neighbors, and as there are differences in mentality and culture, the decision for greater commitment to the Asia-Pacific region was clearly something that we could not achieve simply by forming a team within our existing Economic Development Division. This is why, in January 1986, an Asia Pacific Center was founded in its own right.

The Asia Pacific Center--or APC as we call it--is designed to be more than a mere business promotion office. It has been conceived as a focal point for all those in the business community interested in the Asia-Pacific region. First of all, we have the information side. Today, problems arise, more often than not, through an oversupply of information. The APC's task is to filter that information and tailor it to the inquiring customer's needs. Then we can assist with the formal contacts either by naming business partners or helping to make the introductions in Cologne or the rest of Germany, for example, when a foreign delegation is visiting Germany or when firms in the inquiring customer's line of business have, say, a stand at German trade fairs.

The APC however also works on a reciprocal basis. We aim to serve companies and entrepreneurs from the Asia-Pacific region wishing to do business with the Cologne area. We can help companies from the region prepare for their next trade fair. We rent our office space for single days or even parts of a day at very low prices only to cover our costs. This enables an Asian businessman to consult with potential clients in peace, away from the bustle of the trade fair in an office that is his for the day and completely equipped with telephone, telex, telefax, photocopier, and so on. If he needs to stay longer than expected, we can even accommodate him in our self-catering guest rooms or make a hotel reservation in his name.

Our client structure also complements that of many countries in the Asia-Pacific region where there are also a host of small- and medium-sized companies who would very much like to extend their business relations to Europe if only they had the right partner. What's more, I don't have to tell you that sometimes "small is beautiful." Many of our small- and medium-sized companies are highly specialized in their field, offering technically advanced and even unique, patented products. These are very often the sort of goods that are needed in economies with the comparatively high growth rates of the Asia-Pacific region.

How do we provide information and contacts when we are located in Cologne? Naturally my colleagues and I travel regularly to the Asia-Pacific region; the APC staff has much Asian experience. But for us cooperation is of the essence. As a bank we naturally look to fellow bankers to assist us. As we do not have branches abroad, we consequently pose no threat to the local banks in "poaching" on their customers; on the contrary, we can be of help to their exporting companies.

Our experience has been highly satisfactory, whether the correspondent bank is privately or state-owned. Important for us are the people behind the bank. That is why we regularly visit our colleagues throughout the Asia-Pacific region, making them aware of just what the APC can offer. We like to serve our correspondent banks as we would like to be served by them, basing the relationship on mutual trust, respect, and credibility.

Banking is a field in which the concepts of "public" and "private" often intersect, many banks in the Asia-Pacific region being government-owned. The same can be said of the wide range of trade promotion offices and data banks with which we cooperate in Germany and in the Asian countries. Experience tells us which organizations to approach with each particular type of question. Some organizations are, for example, specialized in developing countries and receive government funding for certain types of projects. Other bodies such as German chambers of commerce abroad can be approached for more general questions. Then again, take the problems involved in legal restrictions. Here sometimes only a governmental body, such as the country's embassy, can provide us with a precise overview of procedure in a particular field.

It should not be forgotten that Cologne itself is an important center for various organizations: the trade fair with an ever-increasing number of foreign exhibitors and visitors, the Central Bureau for Information on International Trade (BfAI); the German Development Corporation (DEG), which provides financing in developing countries and puts up risk capital; the United Nations Investment Promotion Service, particularly for industrial cooperation; the Association of German Industry (BDI); Hermes, the West German export credit agency; and the Carl-Duisberg-Gesellschaft with its staff of 5,000 specialized in training skilled workers and managers in developing countries.

Most important is that the APC's chief aim is true two-way cooperation, in which we have only the interests of our customers and their business partners in the Asia-Pacific region at heart so that both sides can benefit.

Appendix F

The Pacific Islands in the Context of the Pacific Basin

People and their development

The Melanesian countries and territories (Papua New Guinea, Solomon Islands, Vanuatu, New Caledonia, and Fiji) contain about 84 percent of the under six million Pacific Islanders. Polynesia (Tonga, Samoa, Niue, Tokalau, Tuvelu, Cook Islands, French Polynesia, Wallis, and Futuna) contains 10 percent, and Micronesia (Kiribati, Nauru, Marshall Islands, Federated States of Micronesia, Palau, Guam, and Northern Marianas) about 6 percent.

In Polynesia, Micronesia, and New Caledonia, 100 percent of children attend school, and in Fiji a high percentage do, but the proportions are significantly lower in Vanuatu, Solomon Islands, and Papua New Guinea.

The most successful rural training experiments throughout the Pacific (as well as some of the unsuccessful ones) demonstrate that short courses, extension work, and block releases are generally more cost-effective than long-term institutional training. Training is most effective with mature, motivated trainees and trainers (and the latter tend to be more effective when working for voluntary agencies than for governments).

Just over twenty years ago there were no universities in the islands. Now there are eight universities in the islands (not including Hawaii, which has four or New Zealand, which has six) as well as a number of other specialized

This appendix is the summary chapter of a special report prepared by the Institute of Pacific Studies, University of South Pacific.

tertiary institutions. Within another decade there will probably be fifteen universities and a larger number of tertiary institutions in the islands.

A common assumption is that training is best in one's home country or environment. But the opposite assumption--that valuable stimulus and learning is available for those who study in other countries--may be at least as valid in today's world.

The desire to have all jobs in the country held by one's own people is understandable, but the smaller the population, the more difficult this is to accomplish. This is exacerbated by ethnicity, since in many countries various ethnic groups want equitable shares. Populations are typically young so that there is a high dependency ratio and, as the training needs become more intense, the working population has an increasingly heavy burden to carry.

There is a considerable amount of open-market recruiting of specialist staff from the Phillipines, India, New Zealand, and Australia. Free or subsidized staff come mainly from governments or international agencies and are paid, sometimes in part but more commonly in full, by the supplier from their aid allocations.

If cultural diversity is a value--and in many respects it is--the Pacific islands have more of it than any other place on earth. But diversity also has costs. The six million people of the Pacific islands speak 1,200 languages. Preparing school materials and training teachers, for example, constitutes an enormous cost and an only partially surmountable problem.

Studies of hours of work in subsistence societies in various parts of the Pacific show that about twelve to fifteen hours per week was all that was needed on most fertile islands to produce all one's subsistence food, housing, clothing and other necessities of life. Naturally, other activities expanded to use the time. Cultural patterns that emphasized frequent and widespread consumption and distribution derived from a subsistence economy that produced nonstorable foods. In the long term it may well be that some elements of culture are the greatest handicap islanders face in a context of increasing interaction with the dynamic Pacific rim countries.

Corruption is becoming a significant problem in some but not all islands nations. It has a negative effect on the productivity of governments and nations. Nepotism--the favoring by a holder of patronage, his relatives, or others in his interest group--is a problem in some parts of the Pacific.

There have been significant gains in the development of human resources in the Pacific Islands during the past two decades, but the pace of skill development in the industrialized world is even more rapid. If the island nations are to be enabled not only to keep pace, but also to reduce the gap between them and the high-income states of the Pacific rim, much greater emphasis will have to be given to this task by both the islands states and the Pacific rim nations--neither can do it alone.

Economic development

The big problems for the island nations are these: to have rights to their resources (particularly marine resources) properly recognized by larger powers, to conserve the living resources (especially soils, forestry, and marine resources), and to be able to exploit these resources in such a way that they get maximum value for their products over a long period. Being small and lacking in capital and in highly educated manpower, the islands are vulnerable to larger Pacific-rim powers. The resources recognized as economic and the pattern of their utilization are undergoing substantial changes. In the last decade or so forestry, fishing, mining, manufacturing, and tourism have come in to reorient the economy. In the future, sea-bed minerals look promising for eastern Kiribati and the northern Cook Islands, but less so elsewhere.

An essential component of higher productivity is cheaper energy. This is an extreme problem for the Pacific island states. But if renewable energy from sun, wind, and water does develop the way the optimists predict, the islands could become blessed by ample cheap energy. For the immediate future, however, small populations and scattered islands means high production and marketing costs, constraints on what can be sold, and irregular transport.

Land is generally a much under-used resource. The diverse customary tenure systems were designed for a very different context: one without rapid transport, central government, writing or commerce.

The average income is about U.S. $1,100 per head for the South Pacific Commission Region, a level that is low compared with industrialized countries but relatively high for developing countries. Where income levels are high, so is per capita government expenditure. Both are largely due to such special factors as rich mineral deposits (as in Nauru), and high levels of foreign aid, including substantial budgetary assistance or military spending (as in the French and American territories). Overseas remittances from nationals working abroad contribute much more than export earnings for the national income of countries such as Niue, Tokelau, Cook Islands, Tonga, and Western Samoa.

As a proportion of total consumption, subsistence continues to decline despite the fact that every Pacific government aims to increase it for obvious reasons. But achieving that aim is difficult as almost all the models, goals, and aspirations are seen as incompatible with subsistence production.

Islander participation in the ownership and management of business is generally far below that aimed for by governments or hoped for by the public. The reality is a mix of cooperative, state, and private capital, but the proportion of the economy in the hands of cooperatives and state ownership is declining in favor of private enterprise. The proportion of private capital that is foreign owned is generally increasing.

Employment is a coming economic problem, as population is growing rapidly and in many islands exceeds employment opportunities (including those on the land).

Foreign aid is a major component of every Pacific island economy concept Nauru. For several countries more than half the government budget comes from foreign aid. Aid is usually expensive, inefficient, and tied in various degrees to a range of needs of the seller (often called "donor") of the aid. Some aid suppliers are much more demanding than others about what they get back from their aid.

The products that have grown most rapidly in Pacific island states are such public services as education, health, and public works. These are generally welcome, and there is constant pressure on governments for their expansion, despite frequent criticism about lack of efficiency within some of them. In several places the largest increase has been in police and military forces.

The islands are now substantially integrated into the world economy. But along with their smallness and isolation, the limits of natural and human resources leave them vulnerable to vastly larger external forces. If the relationship is to yield optimum benefit to Pacific peoples, there must be a special commitment by rim powers to development of the island states in the fullest sense, and conscious avoidance of the temptation to exploit their vulnerability.

Trade

The main form of trade for many of the smaller Pacific countries is trading political rights for money or other material resources. This major market is created by the Cold War and rivalry between two power blocs. The superpowers and their allies want political support, access for their warplanes and warships as well as (in some cases) space for military bases, and denial of these things to whomsoever the trading power designates as the enemy at the particular time (this of course changes according to the interest of the major power concerned). This situation of maximal dependences is of course the result of "independence," that is, countries have certain rights which others want them to pursue in particular ways. This is a generally more profitable trade than selling primary produce or manufacturing.

The balance of trade of the region is always in deficit. Nauru, American Samoa, and occasionally Papua New Guinea and the Solomon Islands are the only countries that continually have a positive balance-of-trade, through the considerable revenue they receive from the export of phosphate, minerals and canned fish. All other countries have enormous balance of trade deficits which are made good by invisible earnings from tourism, remittances, and aid.

Intraregional trade plays only a very small part in the overall trading patterns in the region.

Tourism offers the best prospects for short-term economic growth, but it is vulnerable to many extraneous pressures form currency fluctuations to hurricanes (though most Pacific islands products are equally vulnerable). Tourism is not as profitable agriculture in terms of value added, employment creation, or income distribution. Nevertheless, tourism has grown in several countries as a source of foreign exchange and employment.

Another area of growth has been in what are called "tax havens," "offshore finance centers," or "international finance centers." In brief, small countries with limited resources guarantee secrecy and no tax in return for licensing fees, a royalty on deposits, and other spin-offs.

Technology

The island states are building relevant data collection and processing facilities, but the major rim powers are accumulating (and sharing between them) data on the islands even more quickly. Information manipulation by big powers (from use of public media to spying) let alone economic or military intervention, could (and probably would) topple any island government that adopts policies unacceptable to the major rim powers.

The two basic systems for long-distance communications in the Pacific are satellites and undersea cables. Satellites radically changed the situation for the South Pacific Islands, because satellite communication is cost-insensitive to distance and maintenance costs are lower than for terrestrial systems.

Each independent Pacific country has a state-owned broadcasting system, as do the French Pacific territories. In addition, privately owned stations operate in some countries and territories. The local stations carry a lot of foreign programs; most are supplied free and therefore carry some element of propaganda or goodwill for the supplier--usually a government with interests in the islands (especially Voice of America, Radio Australia, and to a lesser extent, various others).

Television began with French government broadcasts in New Caledonia and French Polynesia, which may soon have several private stations. American Samoa, Guam, and the U.S. Trust Territory rely on American-based systems. Since independent countries generally eschewed television until video became so prevalent and external pressures to install television so pervasive, a rapid change is in progress.

Despite all the developments in radio and television, print is still the major medium for many people. The small newspapers are locally owned by governments, churches or local businessmen; the larger ones are owned by Australians, Americans or the French. A few magazines are locally produced, but most are from the United States, and to a lesser extent, Australian and French sources. Religious printed matter is abundant in the islands, most of it from American and Australian sources. School curriculum materials are national in some degree, but overwhelmingly from the United States, France, Australia, New Zealand, and the United Kingdom.

Aviation technology is characterized by small aircraft that must be capable of flying relatively long distances, with one or a few of any particular type of aircraft per airline, each requiring its own technical personnel. Fares and freight rates are very high, and most of the airlines have serious financial problems. Many of the same principles apply with shipping.

Despite the very small numbers of cars and other vehicles, every manufacturer wants to be represented everywhere. So small countries have a very wide range of makes and models, making costs high, parts stocks low, and mechanical skills for this wide range of equipment very constrained.

Regional cooperation and competition

Political units in the Pacific are the smallest in the world, with twenty-two governments for two million people, or forty-two if one adds the provincial governments of Papua New Guinea, each with its own premier and ministers. The seventeen countries and territories of Micronesia and Polynesia (excluding New Zealand and Hawaii) average only 50,000 people each, and those of Melanesia (excluding Papua New Guinea and Fiji) only 190,000. Political structures are more diverse here than for any equivalent population in the world.

Federation was seen by some people in the 1940s and 1950s as the best solution for the Pacific Islands once the colonial powers withdrew. None of the proposals came to fruition, and none is likely to. The people are diverse, the cultures different, the distances vast, and a federal government would add a large new burden of expense. Moreover federation would curtail independence, and reduce the number of attractive jobs as members of parliament, cabinet ministers, or heads of even tiny governments.

The independent constitutions of the Pacific nations are all observed, the only region of the Third World where this is generally so. The only exception is Fiji, where the constitution was abrogated by a military coup on May 14, 1987.

The independent governments have generally operated at a high level of integrity by world standards, though recent years have seen some tarnishing of that integrity by some leaders. External pressures in particular are likely to lead to further erosion in the coming years. The pressures are not only from foreign governments and transnational corporations, each pursuing its respective interests, but also from international thugs and confidence men, have already taken in a disturbing number of Pacific governments and leaders. We may come to look back on the 1970s as the high point in Pacific Islands independence.

By world standards regional cooperation among the Pacific countries and territories has achieved a great deal in a short time. Over 250 regional organizations now operate in the Pacific; a generation ago there were almost none. In addition to the vital role of governments, regional religious bodies, business and worker associations, learned and professional societies, and cultural, sporting, and other organizations constitute the network of cooperation and interaction on which a significant degree of Pacific unity has already been built.

On the other hand regional cooperation is constrained by national interest (leaders get their positions through national votes, not regional ones), by bilateral pressures from industrialized nations on the Pacific rim, by the absence of major common external threats, and by the difficulty of applying sanctions to enforce compliance with regional agreements. But by the late 1970s it was becoming clear to the other countries that Fiji's role in regional cooperation was being used in such a way that, while the main costs of most forms of regional cooperation were being paid by external donors and were intended for the equitable benefit of all island countries, Fiji was the main beneficiary.

The spreading of regional institutions is likely to be predominantly westward. Many people are just waking up to the reality that the growing strength lies in the Pidgin-speaking nations (Papua New Guinea, Solomon Islands, and Vanuatu).

Foreign trade unions have some effect in larger islands, but as the Pacific is mainly rural this influence is not yet major. External religious influences, tend to be mainly fundamentalist Christian and politically untraconservative, though Islam is being actively promoted in Irian Jaya, Fiji, New Caledonia, and even Tonga, whose constitution forbids non-Christian religions.

External involvement of all kinds on the Pacific increased dramatically by 1985, particularly regarding strategic issues. It is not likely to decrease in the foreseeable future, and will lead to increases in every activity from subsidies to congruent religious organizations, trade unions, women's groups, and media, as well as direct action in trade, education, government, and even spying. "Strategic denial" becomes a cover for a wide-ranging pattern of penetration and manipulation.

How far Pacific governments can coordinate their leverage in responding to big powers remains a major question for the coming decade, though the 1980s has seen a significant reduction in independence and greatly increased external penetration and manipulation.

Index

Participants in Global Community Forum, 1987

Aiono Fanaafi Le Tagaloa   **Western Samoa**
        Member of Parliament, Western Samoa

Rasheed A. Ali   **Fiji**
        Managing Director, Fiji Sugar Corporation, Limited

Chelliah Sachith Ananthan   **Japan**
        Senior Adviser, Yuasa Battery Co., Ltd., Sri Lanka

Ray Anderson   **Canada**
        President, Asian Pacific Foundation of Canada

Hiroshi Aoki   **Japan**
        Features Section, *Asahi Newspaper*

Pilar Armanet   **Chile**
        Director, Institute of International Studies,
        University of Chile

Eiichi Baba   **Japan**
        Coordinator, Foundation for Advanced Information
        and Research

Richard A. Boyd   **United Kingdom**
        Lecturer in Far Eastern Politics, School of Oriental
        and African Studies, University of London

John F. Boyle   **Western Samoa**
    General Manager, South Pacific Investment Corporation, Ltd.

Peter Corterier   **West Germany**
    Secretary General, North Atlantic Assembly

Ronald Crocombe   **Cook Island**
    Professor, University of South Pacific

Hasyim Djalal   **Indonesia**
    Director General for Research and Development,
    Department of Foreign Affairs

Robert E. Driscoll   **United States**
    President, US-ASEAN Center for Technology Exchange

Peter Drysdale   **Australia**
    Executive Director, Australia-Japan Research Center,
    Australian National University

Junko Edo   **Japan**
    Lecturer, Hosei University

Papiloa Foliaki   **Tonga**
    Managing Director, Friendly Island Hotel

Hisataka Fusikuro   **Japan**
    Researcher, International Cooperation Department,
    National Institute for Research Advancement

Faasootauloa Semi Saili   **Western Samoa**
    Minister of Finance

Fata Pito Fa'alogo   **Western Samoa**
    President, Pacific Islands News Association

Norman George   **Cook Islands**
    Minister of Foreign Affairs

Francois Godement   **France**
    Research Associate, Institut Francais des Relations
    Internationales

Seung-Soo Han   **Korea**
      Professor, Department of Economics,
      Seoul National University

Takako Hattori   **Japan**
      Steering Committee Member of GCF '87

'Ilaisa Futa Helu   **Tonga**
      Director, Atenisi Institute

Hiroyasu Higuchi   **Japan**
      Assistant to Secretary General, Association for
      Promotion of International Cooperation

Osamu Hirose   **Japan**
      Principal Management Consultant,
      Stanford Research Institute International

Eni F. Hunkin   **American Samoa**
      Lieutenant Governor

R. Gordon Jackson   **Australia**
      Chairman, Australian Industry Development
      Corporation

Toshio Kosuge   **Japan**
      Professor, University of Electro-Communications

George Kozmetsky   **United States**
      Executive Associate for Economic Affairs,
      The University of Texas System

Ronya Kozmetsky   **United States**
      President, RGK Foundation

Lau Teik Soon   **Singapore**
      President, Singapore Institute of International Affairs

Le Tagaloa Pita   **Western Samoa**
      Minister for Economic Affairs, Trade, Commerce,
      Industries, Tourism, Statistics, Post Office, and
      Telecommunication and Broadcasting

Charles Lepani   **Papua New Guinea**
      Director, Pacific Islands Development Program

Maiava Iulai Toma   Western Samoa
    Secretary to Government, Ambassador to UN

Colin James Maiden   New Zealand
    Vice Chancellor, University of Auckland

Yoshiro Matsuda   Japan
    Manager, Travel Department, Pacific
    International Japan, Ltd.

Hiroshi Matsumoto   Japan
    Executive Director, Association for Promotion
    of International Cooperation

Shigeo Matsutomi   Japan
    Deputy Director, Oceanian Division, European and
    Oceanic Affairs Bureau, Ministry of Foreign Affairs

Achmad K. P. Mocktan   Indonesia
    Graduate School of International Relations,
    International University of Japan

John McMillan   United States
    Professor, Graduate School of International Relations and Pacific
    Studies, University of California, San Diego

Misa Foni Retzlaff   Western Samoa
    Attorney General

Kimitada Miwa   Japan
    Professor, Sophia University

Kei Mori   Japan
    Professor, Department of Administrative Engineering,
    Faculty of Science and Technology, Keio University

Ronald A. Morse   United States
    Secretary, Asia Program, Woodrow Wilson International
    Center for Scholars

Resio Moses   Federated States of Micronesia
    Governor, State of Ponape

Motu'ahala S. K. Fakasiieiki   Tonga
    General Secretary, Pacific Conference of Churches

Hiroshi Nakajima Japan
  Executive Director, Pacific Society

Masanori Nakamura Japan
  Vice President, International Affairs,
  Japan Air Lines Co., Ltd.

Sampson Ngwele Vanuatu
  Assistant Manager, Transpacific Financial
  Services, Ltd.

Toshiaki Ogasawara Japan
  President, NIFCO Inc.

Toshio Oishi Japan
  Owner, Pacific International Group

Keisuke Okada Japan
  Assistant News Editor, *The Japan Times*

Yujo Okano Japan
  First Secretary, Embassy of Japan to New Zealand, Western
  Samoa, and Cook Island

Yoshio Okawara Japan
  President, Association for Promotion of International
  Cooperation

Saburo Okita Japan
  Chairman, Institute for Domestic and
  International Policy Studies

Palauni Tuiasosopo American Samoa
  Secretary General, South Pacific Commission

Stephen Polonhou Pokawin Papua New Guinea
  Premier, Manus Provincial Government

Elspeth Rostow United States
  Alva Stiles Professor in American Studies and
  Government, The University of Texas at Austin

Walt W. Rostow United States
  Professor of Political Economy, The University of
  Texas at Austin

Francis Joseph Saemala   **Solomon Islands**
        Secretary to Cabinet, Prime Minister's Office

Tatsu Sakai   **Japan**
        Chief Economist, Research Department,
        Institute of Fiscal and Monetary Policy,
        Ministry of Finance

Seizaburo Sato   **Japan**
        Professor of International Relations,
        The Unviersity of Tokyo

Raymond W. Smilor   **United States**
        Executive Director, IC^2 Institute,
        The University of Texas at Austin

Joe Stanley   **Western Samoa**
        Economist, South Pacific Commission

Hiroshi Seita   **Japan**
        Producer, Asahi Video Project

Sun Da Gang   **China**
        Ambassador Extraordinary and Plenipotentiary of
        Peoples Republic of China to Western Samoa

Nozomu Takasaki   **Japan**
        Senior Advisor, Headquarters, Information
        Network Systems Development,
        Mitsubishi Electric Corporation

Masatomo Tanaka   **Japan**
        Assistant Professor, University of
        Electro-Communications

Tau'ili'ili Uili Meredith   **Western Samoa**
        Director, National University of Samoa

Toshihiro Tsubo   **Japan**
        Media Coordinator, Press Alternative

Joses Tuhanuku   **Solomon Islands**
        Secretary General, South Pacific Trade
        Union Forum

Tupuola Efi   **Western Samoa**
　　　Deputy Prime Minister

Joseph C. Walton   **United States**
　　　Assistant to President, M Corp.

Edward White   **United States**
　　　Resident Representative of
　　　United Nations Development Program,
　　　Western Samoa

Yasukichi Yasuba   **Japan**
　　　Professor of Economics, Osaka University

Toru Yano   **Japan**
　　　Professor, Center for Southeast Asian Studies,
　　　Kyoto University

Yoshinobu Yonekawa   **Japan**
　　　Economic Affairs Officer, Department of Technical
　　　Cooperation for Development, United Nations

Visual Telephone Participants in Global Community Forum, 1987

Fritz Hermans   West Germany
    Chairman of the Managing Board, Stadtsparkasse Koln

George Kanahele   United States
    Writer

John D. Rockefeller IV   United States
    United States Senator

Mohammad Sadli   Indonesia
    Chief Economist, Indonesia Chamber of Commerce

Alaelua Saleimoa   Western Samoa
    President, Samoa Cultural Institute

Roniti Teiwaki   Kiribati
    Director, University Extension Center

RGK Foundation   United States

Woodrow Wilson International Center   United States

Contributors

Rasheed A. Ali
Managing Director
The Fiji Sugar Corporation
Fiji

C. S. Ananthan
Senior Advisor
Yuasa Battery Co.
Japan

Peter Drysdale
Executive Director
Australia-Japan Research Centre
Australia National University
Australia

R. Gordon Jackson
Chairman
Australian Industry
  Development Corporation
Australia

George Kozmetsky
Director
IC^2 Institute
The University of Texas
  at Austin
United States

Robert Driscoll
President
US ASEAN Center for Technology
Exchange, Inc.
United States

Faleomavaega Eni F. Hunkin, Jr.
Lieutenant Governor
American Samoa
Eastern Samoa

Va'ai Kolone
Prime Minister
Western Samoa

Charles Lepani
Director
Pacific Islands Development
  Program
East West Centre
Papua New Guinea

C. J. Maiden
Vice-Chancellor
University of Auckland
New Zealand

Hiroshi Matsumoto
Executive Director
Association for Promotion
 of International Cooperation
Japan

Resio Moses
Governor
State of Ponape
Micronesia

John D. Rockefeller IV
Senator
United States

Mohammad Sadli
Chief Economist
KADIN
Indonesian Chamber of
 Commerce and Industry
Indonesia

Lau Teik Soon
Professor
Department of Political
 Science
National University of
 Singapore
Singapore

Toru Yano
Vice President
National Institute for Research
 Advancement
Western Samoa

Kei Mori
Professor
Keio University
Japan

Yoshio Okawara
President
Assocation for Promotion of
 International Cooperation
Japan

Walt Rostow
Professor
The University of Texas at
 Austin
United States

Raymond W. Smilor
Executive Director
IC^2 Institute
The University of Texas at
 Austin
United States

Tau'ili'ili Uili Meredith
Co-ordinator
National University of Samoa
Western Samoa

Yasukichi Yasuba
Professor
Department of Economics
Osaka University
Japan

About the Sponsors

APIC
(Association for Promotion of International Cooperation)

The Association of Promotion of International Cooperation (APIC) is a nonprofit Japanese foundation established in September 1975 under the full support and direction of Japan's Ministry of Foreign Affairs. In order to have Japan's international cooperation make a true contribution to the development of the recipient country, one of APIC's primary objectives has been to perform a "pipeline" function between the government and the private sectors in Japan in furnishing a wide range of information and data on international cooperation to all concerned. APIC also aims to promote "dialogues," holding lectures and meetings as well as to generate overall research works and to deepen the entire Japanese public's understanding of developing countries through "development education." By striving to achieve these objectives, APIC is supporting Japan's effort to undertake its share of responsibility in the international community.

IC^2 Institute

The IC^2 Institute is a major research center for the study of innovation, creativity, and capital--hence IC^2. The institute studies and analyzes information about the enterprise system through an integrated program of research, conferences, and publications.

The key areas of research and study concentration of IC^2 include the management of technology; creative and innovative management, measuring the state of society; dynamic business development and entrepreneurship;

econometrics, economic analysis, and management sciences, and the evaluation of attitudes, opinions, and concerns about key issues.

The institute generates a strong interaction between scholarly developments and real-world issues by conducting national and international conferences, developing initiatives for private- and public-sector consideration, assisting in the establishment of professional organizations and other research institutes and centers, and maintaining collaborative efforts with universities, communities, states, and government agencies.

IC^2 research is published in the form of monographs, policy papers, technical working papers, research articles, and four major series of books.

Institute of the Pacific Studies

The Institute of the Pacific Studies was established in 1976. Its work has been concerned with five major subject areas, all within the social sciences:

1. Social, cultural and economic studies,
2. History and biography,
3. Government and politics,
4. Land tenure policy and development,
5. Language and communication.

Its primary focus is on the eleven countries of the central south Pacific which are served by the University (Cook Islands, Fiji, Kiribati, Nauru, Niue, Solomon Islands, Tokelau, Tonga, Tauvalu, Vanuatu, Western Samoa) but the various projects concerned with the Pacific region cover a wider area (Papua New Guinea, New Caledonia, French Polynesia, the US Territories and various others being in the later but not in the former).

The institute has usually had only two and sometimes three full-time academic staff. The recently-formed Pacific Languages Unit and the Pacific Law Unit, both based in Vila, were set up as separate institutions at the request of IPS and on the basis of an IPS report to carry out and expressed work in these fields formerly done in IPS. In addition to regular university teaching, the institute sees its primary task as the development of skills and confidence and the production of useful research data and publications, primarily by citizens of the region served. This is achieved by facilitating research, writing, consultancy and teaching with IPS participation as appropriate. Results have given us confidence to continue this approach and the IPS Advisory Committee has endorsed this policy.

Over 1,200 authors, mainly Pacific Islanders, have written and published, or are in the course of doing so. In association with the institute, over 100 per year of operation. Consultancy and teaching have likewise been designed to facilitate maximum involvement of regional personnel. This has led to a wide range of inquiries for assistance and for details of the techniques involved, from a variety of people and institutions within the USP region., elsewhere in the Pacific and beyond. A considerable amount of time has been devoted to providing the assistance requested. About 2,400 persons have taken IPS courses. Relative to the size of the academic staff, IPS has taught more M.A. and Ph.D. students than any other section of the university.

Much of the institute's work is carried out in cooperation with the Extension Centers, the Schools and other institutes, or with member governments, regional organization, other universities, and individuals. Their helpful cooperation is gratefully acknowledged, as is that of members of the IPS Advisory Committee.

NIRA
(National Institute for Research Advancement)

To seek viable solutions to the complex, interrelated issues confronting society, interdisciplinary study bringing together a comprehensive range of experts is absolutely essential. The National Institute for Research Advancement (NIRA) was established in 1974 by a special act of the Diet to promote the study of future policies designed to deal with these issues. As a joint public-private organization, NIRA's establishment resulted from the combined initiatives or representatives from government, business, labor, and academic communities.

NIRA is supported by a fund comprised of endowments and contributions from official and private sources.

RGK Foundation

The RGK Foundation was established in 1966 to provide support for medical and educational research. Major emphasis has been placed on the research on connective tissue diseases, particularly scleroderma. The foundation also supports workshops and conferences at educational institutions through which the role of business in American society is examined. Such conferences have been cosponsored with the IC^2 Institute at The University of Texas at Austin and the Keystone Center in Colorado.

The RGK Foundation Building has a research library and provides research space for scholars in residence. The building's extensive conference facilities have been used to conduct national and international conferences. Conferences at the RGK Foundation are designed not only to enhance information exchange on particular topics but also to maintain an interlinkage between business, academia, community, and government.